From glory to ruin

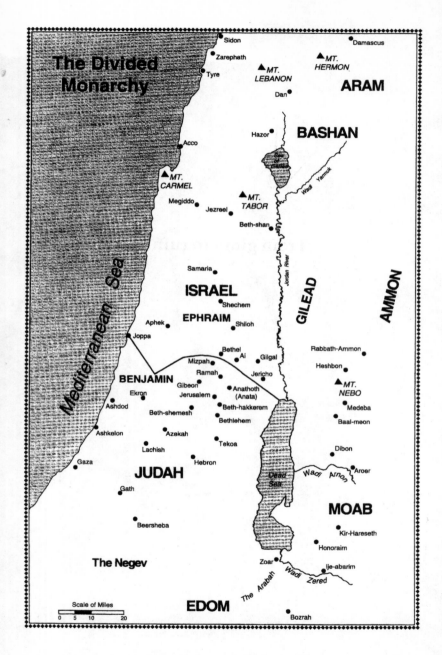

Map of Israel during the divided monarchy

From glory to ruin

1 Kings simply explained

Roger Ellsworth

EVANGELICAL PRESS

EVANGELICAL PRESS
Faverdale North Industrial Estate, Darlington, DL3 0PH, England

Evangelical Press USA
P. O. Box 84, Auburn, MA 01501, USA

e-mail: sales@evangelical-press.org

web: www.evangelical-press.org

First published 2000

British Library Cataloguing in Publication Data available

ISBN 0 85234 451 1

Printed and bound in Great Britain by Creative Print & Design Wales, Ebbw Vale

The following pages are dedicated to
my father-in-law and friend of many years,
Gene Miller.

Contents

Acknowledgements

The chapters of this book were originally presented in sermon form to the congregation of Immanuel Baptist Church, Benton, Illinois. It has been my privilege to walk with these believers. I am constantly encouraged by the love they manifest for the Word of God.

I especially appreciate the encouragement and assistance of my wife Sylvia in preparing these chapters. Special thanks also go to my secretary, Laura Simmons, for bringing to this task her many skills and for sharing in it with her unfailing enthusiasm and pleasantness, and to my friend Paul Orrick for pointing me towards valuable resources.

Roger Ellsworth

Introduction

The books designated as 1 and 2 Kings in our Bibles were, like the books of Samuel, one in the Hebrew Bible. The division was probably made for the purpose of fitting each book on one scroll.

History through the lens of the prophet

Together these books provide a history of the kings of Israel and Judah from Saul to Zedekiah. It would be wrong, however, to think that they are nothing more than history. Consider how various kings are sped by and summarily dismissed. In the light of this it must be said that this is history of a particular sort. It is interpreted history. This is history viewed through the lens of the prophet.

Which of the prophets wrote Kings? Jeremiah has often been identified as the author. Gleason L. Archer Jr. notes, 'One very strong consideration in favour of this conjecture is that there is no mention whatever of Jeremiah himself in the chapters dealing with Josiah and his successors. Apart from modesty on the part of the author, it is hard to account for the failure to mention so important a factor in Judah's history as was the ministry of Jeremiah, her last great prophet.'[1]

1 and 2 Kings could never be mere blow-by-blow history because the people of Israel and Judah were no ordinary people. They were those on whom God had set his heart and with whom he had entered into covenant. They were people who had received divine revelation. They were the people to whom God had announced the coming of the Redeemer.

Furthermore, the kings of Israel and Judah were not kings in the normal sense of the word. They were to recognize that they were only kings on earth, that there was a far greater King, a King in heaven, and they were to rule the people of God with a keen awareness of him and with profound reverence for his person and respect for his laws. They were to rule the people of God on behalf of this great King.

History for a specific readership

Terence E. Fretheim contends that 'Kings is proclamation.'[2] He says it 'was written to have an effect upon readers. The general objective was to bring about change in these readers, to create persons different from what they were before reading took place.'[3]

Who were these readers? The content of the books of Kings leads us to believe that the author wrote for his people while they were in captivity in Babylon. The books of the Kings showed these exiles how they had come to their deplorable state and also prepared them for the future. Their present condition was due to their failure to heed and obey the Word of God. Their future success hinged on their taking a new attitude towards the Word of God, an attitude of submission that embraced its promises and obeyed its precepts.

History with a distinct message

The message of human failure

God had made it clear that nothing was more crucial for the success of his people and their kings than obedience to his laws. In addition to making these laws abundantly clear, the Lord had revealed the disastrous results that would most surely attend the failure to keep those laws (Deut. 28:15-68). God had also made plain that no sin among his people would be more heinous in his eyes and more costly to them than idolatry. It was not 'the luck of the draw' that made this the first of the Ten Commandments: 'You shall have no other gods before me' (Exod. 20:3). Nor was it merely by chance that this commandment should follow: 'You shall not make for yourself a carved image...' (Exod. 20:4).

One would be inclined to think that the force and exceeding clarity with which the Lord had spoken on the matter of idolatry would have removed for ever any possibility of it from the life of Israel. Such an expectation would be ill-founded. While Moses was in the process of receiving the law of God on Mt Sinai, the people were, with the complicity of Moses' brother Aaron, engaged in worshipping a golden calf (Exod. 32:1-10). So deeply engrained in Israel was the propensity towards idolatry that Joshua, the successor of Moses, devoted much of his farewell address to issuing a stinging caution regarding it (Josh. 24:14-23).

When the book of 1 Kings opens, it appears that Israel's flirtations with idolatry are in the past. The long reign of the godly David is coming to a close, a reign which had been remarkably devoted to God, and Solomon is poised to take the throne and lead Israel to unprecedented prosperity and glory.

If anyone should have been immune to the seductive allure of idolatry, it was Solomon. In addition to the law of Moses, Solomon enjoyed the benefit of an explicit warning from his father (1 Kings 2:3) and a message from the Lord himself (1 Kings 9:4-9).

But Solomon shockingly failed to heed these warnings and plunged the nation into idolatry and in so doing took his kingdom from glory to ruin. This leads us to one of the primary purposes of the author of 1 Kings — that is, to show his people that their idolatry had led them into captivity and to call them to a sincere and deep repentance of it. David M. Howard, Jr. writes: 'The sins of the kings and the people are recorded in great detail, not out of a perverse delight in sin and punishment ... but rather as reminders of the people's sins, as warnings to the present exilic generation.'[4]

The message of God's sovereign purpose

1 Kings is not only a book about human failure. It is also a book about God's sovereign purpose. His purpose cannot be thwarted and defeated by human disobedience. Fretheim observes: 'God is the subject of more verbs in these narratives than we may be used to; certainly no modern history is like this.'[5]

God's purpose in human history is unmistakable. It is to bring eternal salvation to his people through his Son, Jesus Christ. This purpose was in place before the world began, and the Old Testament era is an integral part of it. The Old Testament is not just a collection of unrelated documents, a disjointed and piecemeal history of a nation, or a narrative of man's search for God. It is God pointing his people to the coming of his Son.

God had graciously made David part of this plan. He had promised to establish David's throne for ever (2 Sam. 7:16).

Only Christ could fulfil this promise. He sprang from David's line but, unlike David's other sons, Christ will never cease to reign. He is reigning even now in the hearts of his people and will continue to reign for ever.

In the long centuries of the Old Testament, there were many times in which it appeared that God's promises regarding Christ would fall to the ground, The author of 1 and 2 Kings lived after terrible devastation had settled upon the people of God. The Babylonian invasion of 586 B.C. had left the city of Jerusalem in ruins along with the glorious temple built by Solomon. And a very large portion of the population had been deported to far-off Babylon.[6] All of this constituted a most serious challenge to faith. How, in the light of all the ruin and devastation, could the promises of God be true? Had God failed? Did the people of God have a future?

Our vantage-point allows us to answer those questions. We know that despite seemingly insurmountable challenges, God in wisdom and grace so sustained his purpose and fulfilled his promises that Christ not only came, but came in 'the fulness of the time' (Gal. 4:4); that is, at exactly the time God had foreordained.

As we study 1 Kings, we shall have plenty of opportunities to rejoice in the sovereign faithfulness of God and even have occasion to find glimpses of Christ himself.

A message for today

It is all very well to suggest that 1 Kings is a book about human failure and about God's sovereign purpose. The question of keenest interest to most people is this: is 1 Kings a book for today? And the answer is, of course, that it is. The same God who called for the complete devotion of Israel of old calls for the same from his people today. The same God who would not countenance devotion to false gods will brook no rivals today. The God who strongly warned about the calamitous effects of prolonged disobedience still calls his people to love his law and govern themselves according to it. And the same God who could not be thrown off course by man's sins is the God who calls for our wholehearted, unwavering trust today. As he sent Christ the first time to provide salvation, so he will send him again to wrap up human history and to bring his people home. We can and must, therefore, walk with the buoyant step of those who have a certainty born of the knowledge of a God who never fails.

Table of kings

	Israel		*Judah*
Jeroboam I	930-909	Rehoboam	931-913
Nadab	909-908	Abijam (Abijah)	913-910
Baasha	908-886	Asa	910-869
Elah	886-885		
Zimri	885		
Tibni	885-880		
Omri	885-874	Jehoshaphat	873-848
Ahab	874-853		
Ahaziah	853-852	Jehoram	853-841
Joram	852-841	Ahaziah	841
Jehu	841-814	Athaliah	841-835
Jehoahaz	814-798	Joash	835-796
Jehoash	798-782	Amaziah	796-767
Jeroboam II	793-753	Azariah (Uzziah)	792-740
Zechariah	753-752	Jotham	750-732
Shallum	752		
Menahem	752-742		
Pekahiah	742-740		
Pekah	752-732	Ahaz	735-715
Hoshea	732-723	Hezekiah	715-686
		Manasseh	696-642
		Amon	642-640
		Josiah	640-609
		Jehoahaz	609
		Jehoiakim	609-598
		Jehoiachin	597
		Zedekiah	597-586

1.
God's purpose prevailing

Please read 1 Kings 1:1-53

The issue was of immense and vital importance. Who would succeed David as King of Israel? David appears to have considered the matter settled. His successor was to be Solomon, the son of Bathsheba. Although this decision had not yet been announced to the nation (1:20), it was evidently common knowledge within the king's family (1:17,30) and among his closest associates (1:11-13). It was quite obviously known by another of David's sons, Adonijah. The fact that Adonijah invited to his 'coronation feast' all his brothers except Solomon (1:9-10) tells us everything we need to know. It was true that Adonijah was the oldest living son and that the custom in other nations was for the eldest son to succeed his father, but this custom was not yet in place in Israel, which had, on the contrary, a very strong tradition of God bypassing the elder to elevate the younger (Gen. 25:21-23; 1 Sam. 16:1-13). What mattered in Israel was not that the eldest be honoured, but that God be honoured.

But Adonijah did not care what his father had determined. He did not allow for the possibility that his father's choice had been informed and guided by God himself. It made no difference to him that his father had made his choice as the covenant head of the covenant nation, that his father had walked with God in an extraordinarily intimate way. There was no

room in Adonijah's head for God, for David or for Israel because his head was already full — full of himself and ambition.
The author writes, **'Then Adonijah the son of Haggith exalted himself, saying, "I will be king"'** (1:5).

Filled with himself and set upon exalting himself, Adonijah
concocted his elaborate scheme to lay claim to the throne. He
began by conferring with Joab, the captain of David's army,
and Abiathar the priest (1:7). Joab and David had long been at
odds with each other on several counts, and Joab's slaying of
David's rebellious son, Absalom (2 Sam. 18:14), had so
widened the rift that it could never be bridged. Abiathar's de-
fection is not as easy to understand. Perhaps, as several commentators suggest, it was due to jealousy of Zadok, who had
been placed ahead of him. After consulting with these men,
Adonijah proclaimed a great feast (1:7,9).

All of this has a very familiar ring to it. Adonijah's brother
Absalom had acted in a similar fashion when he sought to
overthrow his father (2 Sam. 15:1-14).

The reality of evil within the church

Adonijah's failed scheme speaks powerfully to us about the
reality of evil within the church herself. We must never lose
sight of the fact that Adonijah and his cohorts carried out their
plan within the context of the covenant nation of Israel. The
modern-day successor to Israel is the church of the Lord Jesus
Christ (Rom. 2:28-29; 9:6-8; Gal. 4:28). We expect evil in
society in general, but we have a tendency to think the church
should be exempt from it. Alas, she is not! Adonijah was guilty
of several evils. He rejected the will of God concerning his
brother Solomon. He sowed the seeds of discord in the nation
of Israel. He gave way to his pride and ambition.

The author's account of Adonijah suddenly leaps from the page. The very evils of which he was guilty are still found in the community of faith today. It is not at all difficult to find such rebellion against God's will and his truth. Nor is it difficult to find discord, pride and ambition.

The problem of evil in the world has always been vexing enough to the children of God. What are we to say about evil within the church? Some are quick to say the presence of evil within the church completely discredits her and her message. The truth is rather that in a sense it confirms her. The Lord Jesus Christ assured his followers that evil would exist in the context of the church while she is in this world. A glorious day is coming in which the Lord will finally deliver the church from every last vestige of evil, but while she is in this world she must endure it.

The proper response to evil within the church

The reality of evil in the church does not mean that the saints of God are to give in to it, any more than David and his followers gave in to the evil of Adonijah. They rather responded to the evil in their midst with wisdom and discernment.

Nathan

The prophet Nathan emerges from this account as one who acted with great wisdom. Ronald S. Wallace observes: 'We must give full credit to Nathan for his alertness. He realized that God had placed him in a key position in this very acute and fateful situation. He had to be continually on the watch against those whose ways were a danger to the truth. He had to take full responsibility in the crisis, to begin to act alone.'[1]

God has often defeated evil by causing one person to realize that he or she was in a strategic position and therefore must act for God and for his truth. Mordecai convinced Esther to take a stand for right with words that have motivated and energized the saints of God down through the ages: 'Yet who knows whether you have come to the kingdom for such a time as this?' (Esth. 4:14).

No one has ever been more discerning about evil and more steadfast in standing against it than Daniel. He recognized that God had placed him in a strategic position in Babylon and heroically resisted its evil and stood for God. Martin Luther recognized his strategic position and stood for God's truth when no one else dared to do so. May God help us to do as these saints did. We are not lacking in evil these days, but we are sorely lacking in discerning saints.

David

David can be faulted in two respects. He had been much too soft with Adonijah, even to the point of never rebuking him for any evil (1:6). David can also be faulted for not making his choice of Solomon more vigorously and widely known. But while we acknowledge these faults, we must also credit him with acting wisely and decisively when he learned of Adonijah's scheme.

Bathsheba's plain declaration that **'the eyes of all Israel'** were upon David to settle the matter of succession (1:20), her prediction that she and Solomon would be considered **'offenders'** if Adonijah came to the throne (1:21), and Nathan's confirmation of the developments (1:22-27) achieved their desired result. The old, doddering king sprang into action. After assuring Bathsheba that he had in no way changed his original pledge regarding Solomon (1:28-31), he called upon Zadok (a priest), Nathan (a prophet) and Benaiah (a soldier) to have

Solomon ride on the king's mule to Gihon where Zadok and
Nathan would anoint him and proclaim him king (1:32-35),
assignments which they enthusiastically performed to the letter (1:36-40).

An example to be followed

The wisdom of Nathan and David alerts us to how we should
respond to evil. Some Christians take a fatalistic view of it.
Saying, 'What will be will be,' they blissfully excuse themselves from responsibility. Some Christians are exceedingly
naïve about it. Never able to see danger, they seem eager to
accommodate every new trend. Meanwhile our Lord continues to call his people to be as wise as serpents and as harmless
as doves (Matt. 10:16). We are to discern evil and stand against
it. We are called to see the subtlety of it and the terrible dam-
age it creates.

One wonders if the author of 1 Kings did not begin with
this account so his readers, now exiled in Babylon, would think
long and hard. Adonijah had been prevented from coming to
the throne because Nathan and David had discerned the evil
and had firmly resisted it. The nation's subsequent failure to
do the same was the reason for the exile.

The defeat of evil

Casual observers of the events described in this first chapter
might be inclined to ascribe Solomon's accession to good for-
tune. If Nathan had not heard of the scheme and had not taken
quick action, Adonijah could have succeeded. David had a far
different view of things. According to Jonathan's report to
Adonijah, David had attributed Solomon's accession to God
(1:48).

As far as David was concerned, God had been at work in the midst of this situation to perform his will. This may seem to be a surprising assessment. All through the account of Adonijah's evil scheming, God is apparently absent. As we read we could very well find ourselves inclined to cry: 'Where is God?'

When the whole episode comes to an end, David affirms that God was involved all along. For a while he gave Adonijah free rein, but then he stepped in and put Solomon on the throne. God's way of handling evil is always puzzling to us. Why did God ever allow Adonijah's evil to progress? Why did he not snuff it out at the beginning? One answer must be this: God allowed Adonijah to show his true colours so that no one could finally question whether Solomon was indeed the right choice. Ronald S. Wallace perceptively notes: 'It is characteristic of the way God deals with opposition to his rule that he often allows his opponents full scope to express what is in their minds and hearts so that there may be no doubt that in the end they deserved the punishment they received. He thus allows evil movements often to break out and ripen in order to show their true nature before they are finally crushed.'[2]

A picture of God and his anointed King

This account of Adonijah's vain attempt to seize the throne may very well cause us to think of the Second Psalm. There we find that, just as David had designated Solomon to be King of Israel, so God has designated a king. There can be no doubt about the identity of this king. It is none other than God's own Son, as the psalm itself makes clear (v. 12). In the book of Acts, the apostles referred to this psalm. There was certainly no doubt in their minds that the anointed King of whom the psalm speaks was the Lord Jesus himself (Acts 4:23-28).

As we look further at the psalm we discover yet another parallel. Just as David's designated king, Solomon, was resisted and opposed by Adonijah and his followers, so God's designated King, Jesus, is resisted and opposed by many. And as Adonijah and his supporters thought they could circumvent David's designated king, so those who oppose God fancy that they can successfully resist him and his Christ. The psalmist portrays these opponents as plotting 'a vain thing' (v. 1) and their kings as setting themselves and taking counsel together (v. 2). The point of their consultations is how to overthrow God's anointed King. They say of God and his anointed: 'Let us break their bonds in pieces and cast away their cords from us' (v. 3).

How does the Lord God respond to all their raging and plotting? Does he call an emergency session of the heavenly cabinet? Does he worry or become agitated? Does he fly into a panic? Here is the psalmist's answer:

He who sits in the heavens shall laugh;
The LORD shall hold them in derision.
Then he shall speak to them in his wrath,
And distress them in his deep displeasure:
 'Yet I have set my king
On my holy hill of Zion'

(Ps. 2:4-6).

God has already done the very thing his enemies most want to prevent. He has already declared Christ to be King, and nothing will ever be able to change that. Charles Spurgeon is correct: 'Jehovah's will is done, and man's will frets and raves in vain. God's Anointed is appointed, and shall not be disappointed.'[3]

All that is left for God's enemies, then, is to cast themselves upon the mercy of God. They are called upon to 'be wise' (Ps. 2:10) by not nursing hopes of succeeding against

God. They are commanded to 'serve the LORD with fear' (v. 11), that is, recognize his sovereignty and greatness and bow before him in awe and worship. They are urged to 'rejoice with trembling' (v. 11), that is, to recognize that their happiness and joy are to be found, not in resisting God, but rather in trembling in awe before him. They are told to 'kiss the Son' (v. 12), that is, show true affection to God's Anointed. And they are assured that they will 'perish in the way' if they refuse to do these things. Those who refuse to submit to Christ will some day be cut off while they are still walking in the way of rebellion. They will be going along in their hatred and spewing out their venom against God, and he will suddenly step in and cut them off. They will then find that they have not defeated God's Anointed, but have only succeeded in kindling his wrath (v. 12).

2.
Solomon established

Please read 1 Kings 2:1-46

It was time for David to die. The once mighty king was now a mere shell of his former self. The strength and resiliency of olden days had fled, and the man who was known for his prowess in battle now trembled in his bed (1:1).

As David's life ebbed away his mind was still on his duty. He knew he could still be a source of blessing to his people by carefully instructing and charging his son and successor, Solomon. It was not enough for Solomon merely to have the throne. He must know how to reign from that throne. David, therefore, gathers the remnants of his once mighty strength and speaks solemnly and urgently to his son.

David's charge (2:1-9)

David's charge to Solomon may be divided into two parts: a call to obedience and a call to justice. Howard F. Vos refers to the first of these as a personal charge and the second as an administrative charge.[1]

The call to obedience (2:2-4)

David's call to obedience grew out of his keen awareness that the throne of Israel was like no other. The people of Israel were in a special covenant relationship with the Lord God of heaven. The Lord had freely chosen them as his own. He had delivered them from bondage in Egypt and had established them in their land. He had given them laws by which to conduct themselves. They were to live in such a way that it would be evident to all around them that the God of grace had visited them and blessed them.

The King of Israel played a vital role in this covenant relationship. It was his responsibility to govern as God's representative and in such a way as to hold the nation to her covenant responsibilities. Political leaders today seem to govern largely on the basis of polls. They find out what the majority of their constituents think and then act accordingly. The King of Israel had a constituency of one. He was to concern himself solely with what God desired. As he faithfully served God, he would prove to be the source of immense blessing to his people.

David understood these things, and he knew it was essential for his son to have a firm and unwavering grasp of them as well. We may be sure he had spoken to Solomon on former occasions about these matters. But essential truths can never be rehearsed too often, and dying words have to cut through mere trivialities and meaningless sentiment to that which is truly significant. David could not, therefore, leave this world without again reminding his son of the importance of obedience to God. Nothing was more important to the old saint than that the blessing of God should attend his son and his nation, and nothing was clearer to him than the pathway to God's blessing. It lay in a glad-hearted, ready obedience to God's holy law.

David first called upon Solomon to **'be strong'** and **'prove'** himself to be a man (2:2). Solomon, still very young at nineteen or twenty, was to conduct himself with a maturity beyond his years.

David did not leave his son to speculate about how to do this. Solomon was, therefore, to **'keep the charge'** of the Lord; that is, to do all that the Lord required. He was to **'walk in his ways'**; that is, deliberately and consciously conduct his life according to God's demands. Furthermore, he was to **'keep'** the Lord's **'statutes ... commandments ... judgements ... and ... testimonies'** (2:3). He was to conduct himself according to the directions of the Lord and to govern the nation according to God's laws.

David clearly connected, then, the maturity, or manliness, to which he was calling Solomon with devotion to God and his laws. Solomon's manliness was not, as is so often suggested today, a matter of talking and acting in a 'macho' sort of way, or a matter of athletic prowess. It was a matter of revering and heeding the laws of God. Our definitions of manliness change with the winds of the times, but God's remains the same.

The obedience to which David called Solomon was not an issue that he could be nonchalant and casual about. It was this important: Solomon's success as king would hinge upon it (2:3) as would the perpetuation of David's house (2:4).

The latter benefit creates a difficulty. God had promised perpetuity for the house of David in an unconditional fashion (2 Sam. 7:12-16), but here David makes the promise conditional upon obedience. The problem is resolved by Howard F. Vos: 'The implication is that though the covenant is perpetual, it does not necessarily promise that it will be visibly operative in every generation, regardless of the conduct of kings in the Davidic line.'[2]

All of this may come across to us as being quite unnecessary, but it is far from it. While we are not ruling over kingdoms as Solomon did, we, no less than he, are called to obey God's laws (1 John 2:3-6; 3:4-10,24).

The call to justice (2:5-9)

This brings us to the second part of David's charge, that is, his call to justice. Many contend that David very suddenly and abruptly falls all the way from the top of a mountain to its very bottom. They see him standing on the pinnacle in his plea for obedience to God and then falling from it when he calls for justice. His instructions to Solomon regarding Joab (2:5-6) and Shimei (2:8-9) reflect, in their opinion, a malicious and spiteful spirit. Even his kind words regarding Barzillai (2:7), who came to his aid in the dark days of Absalom's rebellion (2 Sam. 19:31-39), cannot soften or ameliorate what appears to be an unworthy vengefulness on his part.

His call for Solomon to execute *Joab* (2:5-6) is the less troublesome of the two because of the crimes Joab had committed, crimes worthy of death. In addition to murdering two good men (2 Sam. 3:27; 20:9-10), he had sided with Adonijah's bid for the throne (1:7), even though he must have known Solomon was to reign. In charging Solomon to execute him David was, in effect, admitting that he himself had been slack in carrying out justice. It was important for the well-being of the kingdom that Solomon should now send out the unambiguous message that the shedding of innocent blood would be met with swift and severe judgement.

The case of *Shimei* poses a more vexing dilemma (2:8-9). When his son Absalom tried to seize the kingdom, David was forced to flee from Jerusalem. As he fled, Shimei, a devotee of the house of David's predecessor, Saul, had heaped curse after curse upon David (2 Sam. 16:5-8). Shimei deserved to die for his actions, but David, upon his return to Jerusalem, had sworn that he would not put him to death (2 Sam. 19:23).

In calling on Solomon to execute Shimei, David gave evidence that he now considered his pardon to have been rash. He realized that Shimei was not truly sorry for his act and would pose an ongoing threat to his son. In urging Solomon to deal with him, David was not breaking his promise that he himself would not have Shimei executed. It was a matter of Solomon showing in a very strong and emphatic way that treasonous acts would not be tolerated.

David's death (2:10-12)

David died soon after he delivered his charge to Solomon. He had reigned over the tribe of Judah for seven years (2 Sam. 2:4,10-11) and over the entire nation of Israel for an additional thirty-three (2 Sam. 5:1-5). What a blessing he had been to the nation of Israel! He had burst on the scene when Goliath was taunting the army of Israel, had defeated him in battle and delivered his nation from the Philistines. As her king, he had brought the nation to unprecedented power and success. He had defeated her enemies. He had ennobled her worship with psalms. He had ruled with compassion and justice. But now it had all come to an end, and it was time for Solomon to follow the sterling example set by his father.

Solomon's compliance (2:13-46)

Adonijah and Abiathar (2:13-27)

Before Solomon carried out David's instructions regarding Joab and Shimei, he dealt with his brother Adonijah and the priest Abiathar. The former, by requesting for wife the young woman who had ministered to his father (1:1-4; 2:13-18), was essentially laying another claim to the throne, a request that was extremely ill-considered and ended in his being executed (2:19-25). Abiathar the priest, who had also supported Adonijah's bid for the throne, was deposed (2:26-27).

Joab (2:28-35)

Solomon's actions against Adonijah and Abiathar filled Joab with terror. He assumed his life was in danger because of his support of Adonijah. Little did he realize that, in his words to Solomon, David had not even mentioned Joab's association with Adonijah but had focused only on the murders he had committed.

As far as Joab was concerned, his only hope for survival rested in going to the tabernacle, which was probably situated at Gibeon, and laying hold of the horns of the altar. He apparently thought the tabernacle was too holy a place for him to be executed, or perhaps he had learned of Adonijah's being spared on an earlier occasion after doing the same (1:50-53). He was wrong. After receiving instructions from Solomon to carry out the execution, even in the tabernacle, Benaiah proceeded to do so.

Shimei (2:36-46)

After dealing with Joab, Solomon turned his attention to Shimei. He did so in a way that in one sense did not necessitate the latter's death. He demanded that Shimei should not leave the city of Jerusalem for any reason and made it plain that his failure to do so would lead to his death. Shimei could have lived out his days right there in Jerusalem. In another sense, however, Solomon's decree assured Shimei's death. It was only a matter of time until his turbulent, rebellious spirit manifested itself. That time came when Shimei went to Gath to retrieve his fugitive slaves (2:39-46). And Solomon, true to his word, had him executed.

Ronald S. Wallace notes: 'As we read through this whole series of events we are meant to note that they happened by the providence of God rather than by any deliberately made plan of Solomon.'³ Wallace proceeds to observe that both Adonijah and Shimei could have lived in peace within Solomon's kingdom had they been willing to do so, and that Joab essentially declared his guilt before Solomon ever confronted him.⁴

The evils confronting the church

Solomon did all of these things to punish evildoers and to show that his kingdom would be built on justice. It was through these acts of justice that he assured the domestic peace of his kingdom. While Solomon executed Adonijah, Joab and Shimei, he could not execute the evils they represented. Each of these men illustrates for us an evil that is as much a threat to the kingdom of Christ today as it was then.

Adonijah represents the devious, subtle evil that comes cloaked in respectable and innocent language. We do well to associate this particular evil with heretical teachings which so often come in the guise of sweet reasonableness and harmlessness (2 Cor. 11:13-15).

Because Joab's sins were of such public and open nature, murdering his victims in the presence of others, he may be said to represent evil at the other end of the spectrum, that is, the blatant evil that scorns subtlety in its opposition to the things of God. This type of evil often expresses itself in overt persecution of the church.

Shimei may be said to represent sustained evil against the church, evil that never gives up or relents in its hatred of God's truths and his people.

What is the church to do about the presence of these evils? Not invested with the same authority that Solomon enjoyed as the head of a nation, she certainly cannot eliminate her enemies. Rather, she is called upon to love those who hate her.

But while she demonstrates this love, she must also rely upon the Word of God to expose the hatred of her enemies and to give herself the strength to endure their attacks.

We may well wonder how the description of Solomon's dealings with Adonijah, Joab and Shimei affected the exiles in Babylon. For years their nation had been confronted with deceptive teachings, open and unrelenting hostility to the things of God, but very few of their number had taken a strong stand against evil, and the captivity was the result.

The peace of Christ's kingdom

We may also look beyond Solomon to the Lord Jesus Christ, of whom Solomon is in some ways a type. As Solomon was chosen by God to be king long before he actually ascended the throne, so the Lord Jesus, the Second Person of the Trinity, was chosen by God the Father in eternity past to be King over a spiritual and eternal kingdom.

As Solomon used justice to secure the peace of his kingdom, so the Lord Jesus honoured the claims of justice in establishing the peace of his kingdom. By his death on the cross, he himself absorbed the just penalty of God against the sins of his people. Since Christ has taken their penalty, there is no penalty left for them to pay, and they are at peace with God and at peace within. He has made with his people 'a covenant of peace' (Ezek. 34:25) because 'the chastisement' that brought their peace was upon him (Isa. 53:5).

The kingdom of Christ secured by his redeeming death on Calvary's cross will finally come into its final expression. All the enemies of Christ will then be judged and banished and peace shall reign. There will then be no devious Adonijahs, no blatant Joabs, and no perpetually hostile Shimeis. Every last enemy will give way before the glory of Christ and his kingdom.

Those who trust in the LORD
Are like Mount Zion,
Which cannot be moved, but abides for ever...
As for such as turn aside to their crooked ways,
The LORD shall lead them away
With the workers of iniquity.
Peace be upon Israel!

(Ps. 125:1,5).

3.
A good beginning

Please read 1 Kings 3:1-28

After the Constitutional Convention, Benjamin Franklin said to America's citizens, 'We have given you a republic — if you can keep it.'[1]

It is one thing to begin well; it is quite another to end well. The biblical landscape is strewn with accounts of men who began auspiciously, only to falter at the end. Israel's first king, Saul, is a prime example of this. Asa, as we shall have occasion to note in due course, is another. Demas emerges from the New Testament as one who is synonymous with not finishing well (2 Tim. 4:10).

All of these pale in comparison with Solomon. No one had a more impressive beginning and a more dreadful end. 1 Kings chapter 3 lays before us the former. No reign has ever begun more impressively.

As we look at these verses, we are able to discern three very striking features of the opening days of Solomon's reign.

Sincere love and great zeal (3:1-4)

First, we can say that Solomon began with sincere love and great zeal for God. The author explicitly affirms this in these words: **'And Solomon 'oved the LORD...'** (3:3). This love was evidenced by his walking **'in the statutes of his father**

David' (3:3). We are to understand from this that Solomon
began his reign by taking very seriously the dying charge delivered to him by David (2:3) and that he scrupulously adhered to it.

We are living in days in which love to God is often presented as a matter of having our emotions stirred, but Scripture makes it clear that love for God is manifested, not in our
ecstasies, but rather in our obedience (John 14:23-24).

While Solomon was walking in obedience to the Lord's
commands, he was far from perfect. The author makes this
plain by referring to his marriage to Pharaoh's daughter (3:1)
and to his worship at **'the high places'** (3:2-3).

These matters have stirred considerable debate among Bible
students. Many think Solomon was not wrong in doing these
things. On the issue of *his marriage*, they remind us that Israelites were only forbidden to intermarry with those Canaanite
nations they had displaced. They further observe that this Egyp-
tian wife is not included in the list of those who turned Solomon's heart away from God (11:1).

These observations notwithstanding, there can be no doubt
that this marriage was not pleasing to the Lord. We must say
this because Solomon was already married. Before he ascended
to the throne, he had married Naamah, an Ammonitess and
mother of his successor Rehoboam (14:21).

Some argue that in taking many wives Solomon was only
following the accepted custom of his time and that his acceptance of this practice was a means of making important political alliances. But the Lord had revealed from the very beginning that monogamy was his will (Gen. 2:21-24). Furthermore,
he had specifically stated that the kings of Israel were not to
'multiply' wives (Deut. 17:17).

The text itself affirms that *the worship of Solomon in 'the
high places'* was displeasing to the Lord. These were elevated
places, mounds or knolls, on which altars had been built. Such

high places had become very popular in Israel because of a lack of centralized worship. The original tabernacle, first constructed under Moses, was at this time in Gibeon, but the ark of the covenant was in Jerusalem. David could have centralized the worship of Israel. Nothing prevented him from doing so. The Lord had forbidden him to build a temple (2 Sam. 7:1-17), but had not forbidden him to bring the tabernacle to Jerusalem and house the ark in it. But David, great man of God that he was, failed to address this matter.

Solomon knew that the issue of the high places needed to be addressed, but he was willing to let the matter slide until after the temple was built. By that time the high places had become such a snare that the prophets vehemently condemned them.

Solomon's love for the Lord serves as a test for every one of us who names the name of Christ. Does an honest evaluation of our hearts reveal a fervent love for God? Is that love being evidenced by a walk that carefully adheres to the commandments of God? To be sure, Christians are far from perfect and have much over which to grieve, but each child of God ought to be able to testify to a heart that so loves God that there is a strong yearning to obey him and a deep grief when he or she fails to obey.

Profound gratitude (3:5-6)

This leads us to yet another observation about the beginning of Solomon's reign. We can say that Solomon began with profound gratitude to God.

Shortly after he began his reign, Solomon went to Gibeon, which was six miles north-west of Jerusalem. In all likelihood, this constituted a very significant convocation of the entire leadership of the nation. There, at Gibeon, Solomon offered to the Lord a thousand burnt offerings (3:4). These offerings were intended to signify complete devotion to the Lord.

While Solomon was at Gibeon, the Lord appeared to him in a dream (3:5). Here we get a small glimpse of the astonishing grace of God. Solomon, as we have noted, was not perfect in obedience, but the Lord appeared to him just the same. How we should rejoice that the Lord is gracious to us even though we are sinful!

The Lord's visit itself would have been gracious enough, but God manifested his grace even further by saying to Solomon, **'Ask! What shall I give you?'** (3:5).

Solomon's answer is most striking. We would expect to read that he immediately answered the Lord's question, but instead he began to tick off the blessings God had so abundantly bestowed upon his father David and himself (3:6). This shows us the gratitude of Solomon's heart. He recognized that he was where he was, not because of any merit of his own, but rather because God had been gracious to him.

We Christians are not called to reign as Solomon was, but while his task is not ours, his gratitude can and should be. The very same God who had been so kind and gracious to him has also showered his mercy upon us. He has delivered us from the bondage of sin. He has given us right standing before him. He has adopted us into his family. We are blessed beyond our ability to measure. And all the spiritual blessings we enjoy flow to us, not because of any merit of our own, but rather because of the finished work of the Lord Jesus Christ. We function as Christians ought when we are most mindful of these blessings and praising God for them.

Deep humility and a hearty dependence on God (3:7-28)

Finally, we can say Solomon began with deep humility and a hearty dependence on God.

After thanking God for his blessings, Solomon proceeded to answer the question the Lord had put to him. He realized he was faced with an awesome task. The people of Israel were God's chosen people and the sheer number of them made governing them a daunting task (3:8). In addition to these things, Solomon felt that he was nothing more than **'a little child'** (3:7). His confession, **'I do not know how to go out or come in,'** was the standard way of saying he was inexperienced in leadership. Solomon knew his most pressing need, therefore, was for **'an understanding heart to judge'** so that he could **'discern between good and evil'** (3:9).

God granted this request. And, as another indication of the astonishing nature of his grace, he gave Solomon those things he could have requested but did not: riches, honour and long life (3:13-14).

Solomon's wisdom was soon put to the test. Two harlots had given birth to sons. One lay on hers during the night, smothered him and switched her dead child with the living child of the other woman. The second woman immediately perceived what had been done, but how was she to prove it? She insisted that the two of them go to Solomon.

And Solomon decided the case. He commanded that a sword be brought and the living child be cut into two and one part be given to each woman. The true mother could not bear such a suggestion. She was willing to give up her son rather than see him die. As soon as she began to plead for the life of her son, Solomon had his answer. The child was awarded to this woman, and the news of Solomon's wisdom in administering justice went out across the land.

Solomon's wisdom showed that the two women were exact opposites. It divided them and placed them in their true categories. It showed the one woman to be self-serving, cruel and heartless, and the other to be willing to sacrifice her own desires for the good of her child. In like manner, the Lord Jesus Christ is a divider of men. It was not by chance that his cross was situated between the crosses of two thieves, and that one of these repented while the other did not (Luke 23:39-43).

The primary manifestation of Solomon's wisdom is to be found in the 'wisdom literature' that he produced: Proverbs, Ecclesiastes and the Song of Solomon. 'Wisdom' in these books is essentially insight or discernment. It is knowing how to handle what life brings our way. It is seeing and doing the right thing in whatever situation presents itself. It is making the right choices in life, choices that enable us to reap the good that life has to offer. It is grasping divine reality and bringing it to bear on the issues and circumstances of life.

How do we get this wisdom? We must realize that God is the source of it (Prov. 2:6), and he gives it to those who fear him (Prov. 1:7; 9:10), that is, to those who realize his greatness and majesty, who dread his displeasure and who come to him with a humble and teachable spirit (Prov. 3:7). It is imposs-ible to receive God's wisdom apart from the careful hearing and heeding of his Word.

How sad it is that Solomon himself, after years of embrac-ing God's wisdom and teaching others to do so as well, turned his back on it in his latter years and became very foolish and undiscerning! (11:1-13).

Vital lessons

The main lessons of this episode lie, however, in the vital im-portance of prayer and in the faithfulness of God to his promises.

The vital importance of prayer

The first word the Lord spoke when he appeared to Solomon was 'Ask!' That command had prompted Solomon to ask for wisdom, and it was now evident that Solomon's prayer had been granted. God takes the prayers of his people seriously. Having determined in his sovereign wisdom to use their prayers as means to accomplish his work, the Lord commands his people to pray and stands ready to hear and answer their prayers. We often vex ourselves with 'the problem of unanswered prayer'. Far greater is 'the problem of unasked prayer'. We do not have because we do not ask (James 4:2).

The faithfulness of God

The faithfulness of God also shines out in Solomon's handling of the case of the harlots. The Lord had promised to give Solomon wisdom (3:12), and this case furnished proof that he would be true to his word. How the readers of 1 Kings must have rejoiced over this seemingly small detail! The same Lord who had kept his promise to Solomon had made promises regarding the future of the nation. That future was not to waste away in Babylon and finally come to oblivion. It was rather for their nation to be restored to her land and to be the nation of the Messiah. No matter how bleak their situation appeared, the promises of God could be trusted.

We are able to see from our vantage-point that God did indeed keep his promises to the nation. She was released from Babylon and restored to her land, and the Messiah did come to her. The captivity never nullified the promises of God.

The faithfulness of God is still cause for rejoicing. The Lord has given to us too 'exceedingly great and precious promises' (2 Peter 1:4). Our circumstances may often make these promises seem shaky and insecure, but the same Lord who was faithful to Solomon and to his people in Babylon will be faithful to us as well. Has he promised to be with us and never forsake us? (Heb. 13:5-6). He is with us! Has he promised to hear and answer our prayers? (Matt. 7:7-8). We may pray confidently! Has he promised that his Word will be efficacious

and powerful? (Isa. 55:11). We may proclaim it with bold-
ness! Has he promised to come again and receive us unto himself? (John 14:3). We may keep looking up!

The elements with which Solomon began his reign would
have served him well all through his life and reign. They were
good ingredients with which to begin and with which to end.
Solomon, however, deviated from them and brought much
pain and misery upon his kingdom.

We can learn from him. We can make sure these elements
with which he began are in place in our lives and that they
continue to be in place. In so doing, we will bring the blessing
of God upon our lives and upon the lives of those around us.

4.
Solomon in all his glory

Please read 1 Kings 4:1-34

The third chapter of 1 Kings closes with a specific example of the wisdom of Solomon (3:16-28). The fourth chapter opens and closes by putting that same wisdom on display (4:1-19, 29-34). Between those two sections is a statement about the prosperity of Solomon's kingdom (4:20-28). The Lord was abundantly good to Solomon, giving him the wisdom for which he had asked (3:12) and the riches and honour for which he had not asked (3:13).

The sections on wisdom celebrate both Solomon's administrative ability and his intellectual attainments.

Solomon's administrative ability (4:1-19)

His officials (4:2-6)

The priests. Solomon appointed eleven men to serve him in various capacities. Four of these were priests: Azariah (4:2), Zadok (4:4), Abiathar (4:4) and Zabud (4:5). It is somewhat surprising to find Abiathar, the priest who had allied himself with Adonijah, in this group. Perhaps he is included because Solomon had forgiven him and restored him to office. Or, as

some commentators think, Solomon may have only allowed
him to retain the title of priest while he did not officially function as one.

The scribes and recorder. Elihoreph and Ahijah, the scribes,
were charged with caring for the king's correspondence, keeping records and supervising the archives. The Hebrew word
translated **'recorder'** means 'the one who calls, names, reminds, reports'. R. D. Patterson writes of Jehoshaphat, who
filled this role, 'He was in charge of palace ceremonies, the
chief of protocol. He reported public needs to the king and in
turn was the king's spokesman.'[1]

Other officials. Benaiah, who had headed David's special
guard, was commander-in-chief of Solomon's army (4:4).
Azariah was in charge of the district governors (4:5), while
Ahishar had supervision of Solomon's household staff (4:6).
Adoniram was in charge of Solomon's conscripted labour force
(4:6).

His districts (4:7-19)

A further manifestation of Solomon's administrative ability was
his division of the kingdom into twelve districts. The purpose
of this organization was to provide food for the royal household (4:7). Each district was responsible for the provision for
one month of the year. While these districts were the same in
number as Israel's tribes, they were not the same as the tribal
divisions. It is noteworthy that the tribe of Judah is not mentioned here. Howard F. Vos observes: 'Judah's favoured status
accentuated tribal rivalries and contributed to the split that
occurred in Rehoboam's day.'[2]

The prosperity of Solomon's kingdom (4:20-28)

The author follows his description of Solomon's administrative ability with a summary of the prosperity of the kingdom. This prosperity is set forth in terms of the size of population, the comforts enjoyed, the area covered, the provisions made for the court and the level of security.

The size of population (4:20)

Solomon's reign coincided with a population explosion in Israel that saw the people become **'as numerous as the sand by the sea in multitude'**. With this phrase the author is claiming the fulfilment of the promise the Lord had made to Abraham, the father of the nation of Israel, that his descendants would be 'as the stars of the heaven and as the sand which is on the seashore' (Gen. 22:17).

The comforts enjoyed (4:20)

The author depicts the lifestyle of Solomon's subjects by merely saying they were **'eating and drinking and rejoicing'**.

The area covered (4:21,24)

The area over which Solomon reigned finally fulfilled the promises God had made to Abraham about the land that the Lord would give to his descendants (Gen. 12:1-9).

Provisions for the court (4:22-23,26-28)

Such an impressive government required a great number of provisions to sustain it. Estimates of the number of people for

whom Solomon had to provide run from 14,000 to 32,000.
The great number of horses also required abundant provisions.
(Note: many commentators believe the number 40,000 in verse
26 to be the result of a copyist's error and accept the number
4,000 given in 2 Chronicles 9:25 instead).

The level of security (4:24-25)

Solomon's reign was a time of peace for Israel. No enemy
threatened from any side, and the people of Israel **'dwelt
safely'**.

A picture of future glory

In the light of all these things, we have to say these were the
glory days of the Old Testament church. Under the good hand
of God, Israel had reached the pinnacle of blessing. We may
see in these days a glorious anticipation of the glory that yet
awaits the church.

For instance, *the explosion of population* during Solomon's
reign may well cause us to look forward to the fulfilment of
these words from the apostle John: 'After these things I looked,
and behold, a great multitude which no one could number, of
all nations, tribes, peoples, and tongues, standing before the
throne and before the Lamb, clothed with white robes, with
palm branches in their hands, and crying out with a loud voice,
saying, "Salvation belongs to our God who sits on the throne,
and to the Lamb!"' (Rev. 7:9). This numberless throng will
consist of those whom the Lord God chose for himself in eternity past, whom he redeemed from sin through the saving work
of Jesus Christ and called to himself through the work of the
Holy Spirit. These are the true descendants of Abraham because they share his faith (Rom. 4:13-16; 9:6-8; Gal. 3:29).

The security of Israel under Solomon is another detail which causes us to think of the church's future glory. We have only to look again to the book of Revelation to see this. John reports the words spoken to him by one of the elders about the numberless throng he had seen: 'They shall neither hunger any more nor thirst any more; the sun shall not strike them, nor any heat; for the Lamb who is in the midst of the throne will shepherd them and lead them to living fountains of waters. And God will wipe away every tear from their eyes' (Rev. 7:16-17).

Solomon's intellectual attainments (4:29-34)

Having given a summary of the prosperity of Solomon and his kingdom, the author returns to the subject of the king's wisdom. The wisdom he sets forth in these verses goes far beyond the judicial and administrative skills already mentioned. Here the author attributes **'wisdom'** to Solomon. Gleason Archer defines this wisdom as 'a proper discernment between good and evil, between virtue and vice, between duty and self-indulgence ... a skill in the accomplishment of business affairs as well as in the handling of people'.[3]

Solomon also had **'understanding'**. Archer defines this as 'the ability to discern intelligently the difference between sham and reality, between truth and error, between the specious attraction of the moment and the long-range values that govern a truly successful life'.[4]

Finally, Solomon possessed **'largeness of heart'**, that is, a large breadth of interests, some of which are mentioned in verse 33.

Solomon's wisdom was such that he not only surpassed the other wise men of his day (4:30-31), but also commanded the attention of other heads of state who came to draw from his wisdom (4:34).

Solomon expressed much of his wisdom in proverbs and songs (4:32). The book of Proverbs and the Song of Solomon are samples of his numerous writings.

The glory of Christ's kingdom

The summary given above constitutes only a brief glimpse into the glory of Solomon's kingdom, but it is sufficient to compel us to join Matthew Henry in saying, 'Such a kingdom, and such a court... '[5]

The glory of Solomon's kingdom, impressive as it was, cannot begin to compare with the glory of another kingdom, that is, the kingdom of Jesus Christ. Henry observes: 'Never did the crown of Israel shine so brightly as it did when Solomon wore it, never in his father's days, never in the days of any of his successors; nor was that kingdom ever so glorious a type of the kingdom of the Messiah as it was then.'[6]

S. G. DeGraaf makes the same connection between Solomon's kingdom and the kingdom of Christ. He writes, 'This wonderful kingdom of peace was a foreshadowing of a still more glorious Kingdom of peace that Christ would establish one day.'[7]

Henry, DeGraaf and others who find parallels between the kingdom of Solomon and the kingdom of Christ do so for a very good and legitimate reason: Scripture itself connects the two! Psalm 72 is designated as 'A psalm of Solomon', but, in the light of the last verse, which attributes the writing of it to David, it should more properly be given the title, 'A psalm for Solomon'. In this psalm David both prays for God's blessing on his son and prophesies that blessing. One does not go far into this psalm before realizing that it rises to a much higher level than Solomon's reign. Derek Kidner explains: 'As a royal psalm it prayed for the reigning king, and was a strong reminder of his high calling; yet it exalted this so far beyond the humanly attainable (e.g. in speaking of his reign as endless) as to suggest for its fulfilment no less a person than the Messiah...'[8]

The following are some of the parallels between Solomon and Christ:

1. As Solomon's reign was characterized by wisdom, so Christ is the wisdom of God (1 Cor. 1:24). In Christ, the apostle Paul writes, 'are hidden all the treasures of wisdom and knowledge' (Col. 2:3). Christ is both the embodiment and the expression of all the wisdom that is in God. The highest knowledge which any man can possess is to be found in Christ, and the highest act of God's wisdom is the cross upon which Jesus died. There God in wisdom at one and the same time punished sin (thus satisfying God's justice) and provided atonement for guilty sinners (thus satisfying God's grace).

2. As Solomon's kingdom was one of justice, peace and joy, so Christ's kingdom is, in the words of Paul, 'righteousness and peace and joy in the Holy Spirit' (Rom. 14:17).

Regarding the peace of Solomon's kingdom, we should remind ourselves that it came about as a result of the wars of his father David. Jonathan Edwards finds a parallel between David, the man of war, and Christ in his state of humiliation, before drawing the parallel between Solomon, a man of peace, and Christ 'exalted, triumphing and reigning in his kingdom of peace'.[9]

3. As Solomon ruled over other nations, so Christ shall have the heathen for his inheritance (Ps. 2:8).

5.
Preparations for temple building

Please read 1 Kings 5:1-18

The building of the temple dominates the first half of 1 Kings. Chapter 5 relates Solomon's preparations for construction. Chapter 6 focuses on the process of construction. Chapter 7 begins with a description of some of Solomon's other building projects but quickly moves back to the temple and its various furnishings. Chapter 8 describes the dedication of the temple. The sheer quantity of the material devoted to the temple underscores its importance in the life of Israel.

The chapters on construction present us with details of plans, labourers, dimensions, materials and furnishings, so much so that it is possible to become immersed in detail and fail to see the larger picture.

Some of the major aspects of that larger picture emerge in this chapter. This appears to be a 'nuts and bolts' chapter. Solomon first provides the materials for building the temple by entering into an agreement with Hiram, King of Tyre (5:1-12). He then secures the needed labour force (5:13-18). But if we listen closely to this chapter, we shall hear it making some affirmations that take us far beyond the realm of nuts and bolts to truths that are just as valid — and exhilarating — as they were at the time Solomon built the temple.

God is gracious

This chapter includes three distinct and explicit testimonies to
the grace of God.

Solomon's testimony (5:2-6)

The first testimony comes from Solomon himself. He writes
to Hiram, King of Tyre, to enlist the help of the Phoenicians,
who were extremely skilled in such matters. In the midst of his
letter to Hiram he says, **'... the LORD my God has given me
rest on every side...'** (5:4).

Great domestic projects cannot be undertaken and successfully completed when a nation is engaged in warfare. War si-
phons time and resources away from all other concerns. Solomon was under no illusions about how his kingdom had come
to enjoy the peace that made it possible to build the temple. It
was not just a fortunate turn of circumstances. It was rather
because, as he stated, the Lord had given him rest.

God does his work through means, and the means he had
used to provide peace for Solomon's kingdom was Solomon's
father (5:3). David had wanted to build the temple, but the
Lord's purpose for him was to pave the way for his son to
build it by defeating Israel's enemies (2 Sam. 7:1-17).

Hiram's testimony (5:7)

The second testimony to the grace of God is found in these
words from Hiram: **'Blessed be the LORD this day, for he
has given David a wise son over this great people!'**(5:7).

There is no evidence that Hiram ever came to embrace the
God of Israel with a true and living faith, and we do not know
to what degree he understood his own words, but, whether
fully understood or not, they were true. Just as God wrung

speech out of Balaam's donkey (Num. 22:28-30), so here he wrings praise out of a worshipper of other gods.

The author's testimony (5:12)

The author of 1 Kings also adds his own testimony to the grace of God in the building of the temple: **'So the LORD gave Solomon wisdom.'** Solomon, Hiram and the author join their voices, as it were, to attribute both the rest and the wisdom Solomon enjoyed to the Lord.

As we read the New Testament we discover that God is still in the temple-building business. Each believer is a temple which God is building, and the entire church is as well. No individual Christian can ever take credit for his service to God. If he loves God, it is because God loved him before time began. If he desires to serve God, it is because God is at work in him 'both to will and to do for his good pleasure' (Phil. 2:13). If he gives to God, it is because God has first given to him (1 Chr. 29:16). The apostle Paul makes this point splendidly by first asking the question the Lord put to Job: 'Or who has first given to him and it shall be repaid to him?' Paul then turns to give this emphatic answer: 'For of him and through him and to him are all things, to whom be glory for ever. Amen' (Rom. 11:35,36).

If each individual Christian is a product of God's grace, the whole church is as well. The church is not a mere human invention. She is God's. She is the church of the living God (1 Tim. 3:15). She is his building, his field (1 Cor. 3:9), his household and dwelling-place (Eph. 2:19,22) and his flock (1 Peter 5:2). He chose her before the foundation of the world (Eph. 1:4) and gave her to his Son (John 17:6,12), who came to this world and purchased her with his own blood (Eph. 5:25-27). And God will eventually present the church to his Son in the glory of eternity. It is all of God's grace.

God uses human instruments

The grace of God in giving all that is necessary for human service does not negate or eliminate human responsibility. God gave everything necessary for Solomon to build the temple, but Solomon still had to act. This fifth chapter of 1 Kings is largely about Solomon acting: **'Solomon sent to Hiram...'** (5:2); **'Solomon gave Hiram twenty thousand kors of wheat...'** (5:11); **'Then King Solomon raised up a labour force...'** (5:13); **'And the king commanded them...'** (5:17).

The truth is that Solomon is only one among many human instruments in this chapter. The whole is buzzing with activity. Cedars are cut and sent by the Phoenicians, with the help of the Israelites (5:6,10,13-14). Burdens are carried (5:15). Stones are quarried (5:17-18). And all is carefully supervised (5:16). From it all we learn that the God who can work without us has chosen to work through us.

God does not build individual believers by telling them merely to sit back and do nothing. He rather builds them as they give themselves to strenuous and diligent activity, as they read and study his Word, mortify their flesh, pray, worship and continue in the faith.

The Lord also builds his church by working through instruments. He does not tell us to while our time away in idleness as he builds his church. He builds the church through the means he has appointed, of which the primary one is the vigorous preaching of his gospel. When the church abandons the gospel, she abandons the means that God has ordained for building his church. Other means may build the church in numbers and in dollars, but only the means God has appointed can impart spiritual life to dead sinners and truly make them part of God's church. Much of what goes on in many churches today has to be chalked up to dependence upon the flesh. This, as

Abraham discovered, is very effective in producing Ishmaels, but it takes the grace and power of God to produce Isaacs (Gen. 16:1-16; 21:1-21).

God is worthy

Solomon's preparations for the construction of the temple also bear witness to the worthiness of the Lord. Solomon's father David had put the building of the temple in the proper perspective with these words: 'The temple is not for man but for the LORD God' (1 Chr. 29:1).

David was not permitted to build the temple, but he did plan very carefully for Solomon's building of it. As he planned, David kept in mind that the temple was to be a testimony to the Lord's excellence and worthiness. The temple was to be for him. Nowhere did David more clearly express this than in the prayer he offered at his final public assembly:

> Blessed are you, LORD God of Israel, our Father, for
>   ever and ever.
> Yours, O LORD, is the greatness,
> The power and the glory,
> The victory and the majesty;
> For all that is in heaven and in earth is yours;
> Yours is the kingdom, O LORD,
> And you are exalted as head over all.
> Both riches and honour come from you,
> And you reign over all.
> In your hand is power and might;
> In your hand it is to make great
> And to give strength to all.
> Now therefore, our God,

We thank you
And praise your glorious name.

(1 Chr. 29:10-12).

It is not surprising, then, that David prepared so lavishly
for the temple. His testimony was that he had prepared with
all his might (1 Chr. 29:2) because he had set his 'affection' on
the house of the Lord (1 Chr. 29:3). This had led him to lay
aside 3,000 talents of gold and 7,000 talents of silver (1 Chr.
29:4). It was all due to David's unwavering conviction that
the temple was for the Lord who was worthy of the devotion
and worship of his people.

Solomon began his preparations for the temple's construction with the same conviction riveted in his mind. He tells Hiram
that the temple is **'for the name of the LORD my God'** (5:5).
A fuller account of Solomon's letter is recorded in 2 Chronicles. There Solomon is reported as writing:

> Behold, I am building a temple for the name of the
> LORD my God, to dedicate it to him... And the temple
> which I build will be great, for our God is greater than
> all gods. But who is able to build him a temple, since
> heaven and the heaven of heavens cannot contain him?
>
> (2 Chr. 2:4-6).

Such a God deserves nothing but the very best, and David
and Solomon, with that conviction drilled into their hearts,
gave their very best in the planning for, and the building of, the
temple. Because God is no less glorious today than he was
then, we who know him must be as devoted to giving our best
as they were.

6.
Solomon the builder

Please read 1 Kings 6:1 - 7:51

These two chapters present Solomon as a builder *par excellence*. Twice in chapter 6 we are told that he **'built the temple
and finished it'** (6:9,14). Chapter 7 opens by telling us that
he built several buildings which may have constituted a palace
complex. Included were his own residence (7:1), the House of
the Forest of Lebanon (7:2-5), the Hall of Pillars (7:6), the
throne room or Hall of Judgement (7:7), a court inside the
throne room (7:8) and a palace for his wife, Pharaoh's daughter (7:8). All of these buildings were very elaborate and or-
nate, featuring costly, large stones and cedar wood (7:9-12).

Foremost among Solomon's building projects was the
temple of the Lord, the temple for which his father David had
planned and prepared. 480 years after Israel was delivered
from bondage in Egypt, and in the fourth year of his reign,
Solomon began to build the temple (6:1,37). Seven years later
the massive project was complete (6:38). We might find ourselves astonished that it took the Lord so long to put his people
into a position to do this. God's ways seem strangely slow to
us, but there is a purpose in all that he does.

Scripture includes two accounts of the building of the
temple. The one in 2 Chronicles, while similar in many respects
to that of 1 Kings, is much shorter, less than half the size of
that found here.

A temple tour (6:1-10,14-38; 7:15-51)

Perhaps the best way to handle the large amount of information about the temple is to think of ourselves as on something of 'a guided tour', as Michael Wilcock does in his commentary on 2 Chronicles.[1] As we take this tour, we must remind ourselves that Solomon's temple serves as a picture of the New Testament church (1 Cor. 3:16; 2 Cor. 6:16; Eph. 2:21; Heb. 3:6; 1 Peter 2:5).

The temple proper

We begin this tour by imagining ourselves standing in the porch, or **'vestibule'**, of this building (6:3), which is 90 feet (about 27 metres) in length, 30 feet (9 metres) in width and 45 feet (13.5 metres) in height. (If, as some suggest, the royal cubit, roughly equivalent to 21 inches, was used, this would mean that the length was 105 feet, or 31.5 metres, the width 35 feet or 10.5 metres, and the height 52½ feet, or 15.75 metres.)[2]

Solomon's temple was built of stones that were finished at the quarry so that all that had to be done when they were on the site was to fit them into place. The author says, **'No hammer or chisel or any iron tool was heard in the temple while it was being built'** (6:7). John Gill observes that the finishing at the quarry suggests 'that none are to be laid in the spiritual building of the church, but such as are first hewed and squared by the spirit, grace and word of God: or who have an experience of the grace of God, are sound in the faith, and of becoming lives and conversations...'[3] He then adds that the silence at the site suggests that those who have been placed in the church 'should do all they do for the edification of the church in a quiet and peaceable manner, without clamour, contention, jars, and tumults'.[4]

The porch where we imagine ourselves standing measures 15 feet (4.5 metres) in length (6:3), and is the first of the temple's three main sections. It has a large bronze pillar on each side. On the south is the pillar **'Jachin'** and on the north **'Boaz'** (7:15-22). The name of the former means 'He establishes', and the latter 'In him is strength'. These two pillars testified to the divine origin and the stability of God's promises to David.

From the vestibule we enter the sanctuary, or the Holy Place, which was the largest of the three sections (60 feet, or 18 metres, long). The inner sanctuary, or Holy Place, was separated from the Most Holy Place (6:16-20). This room, consisting of a cedar-board floor and walls (6:16) was 30 feet (9 metres) in length and separated from the Holy Place by a heavy curtain, or veil (2 Chr. 3:14). It was the most sacred place of the temple. Here the high priest of Israel entered once a year to make atonement for the sins of the people.

Inside the Most Holy Place were two cherubim (6:23-28), winged creatures with human faces, on either side of where the ark of the covenant would eventually be placed (8:4-9). Their outstretched wings stretched 15 feet (4.5 metres) upwards, half the height of the Most Holy Place.

The courtyard

We make our way back to the vestibule and stand looking out towards the courtyard. While there our eyes are drawn to **'the Sea of cast bronze'** (7:23-26) which provided the water for the priests to wash themselves (2 Chr. 4:6).

This huge vessel (15 feet, or 4.6 metres, in diameter; 7½ feet, or 2.3 metres, in height; and 45 feet, or 13.7 metres, in circumference) was capable of holding a huge amount of water. The author of 2 Chronicles puts the capacity at 3,000 baths (approximately 17,000 gallons, or 64,350 litres), while the author of 1 Kings puts it at 2,000 baths (approximately 11,500 gallons, or 43,500 litres). Eugene H. Merrill suggests that the former may refer to total capacity and the latter to the actual amount kept in the Sea, namely, two-thirds of its capacity.[5]

Such a large reservoir required a very solid foundation. This was provided by twelve bronze bulls, sets of three facing in each direction with their hindquarters towards the centre (7:25).

Also visible in the courtyard are **'ten lavers of bronze'** (7:38-39), five of which were placed on the north side of the Sea and five on the south. These lavers rested on **'carts'** or trolleys (7:27-37). These basins, each containing forty baths of water (approximately 230 gallons, or 870 litres) were used to wash the animals that were to be sacrificed.

In addition to all these things, there were various pots, shovels and bowls (7:40,45), all of which were made of burnished bronze by Huram, or Hiram. This man, not to be confused with the King of Tyre (5:1-12), was half-Israelite. His mother was **'a widow from the tribe of Naphtali'** and his father was **'a man of Tyre'** (7:13-14). Eugene H. Merrill says of him: 'He was ideally suited to the task since he was half-Israelite and thus sympathetic to the project and half-Phoenician and thus skilled in its execution.'[6]

The temple testimony

We have attempted to visualize the temple that Solomon built. But let's suppose for a moment that we could hear it talk. What would it say?

The temple says, 'Glory'

One word we would certainly hear from the temple is 'glory'. Centuries later, when the Jews had returned from their captivity in Babylon and were in the process of rebuilding the temple, the prophet Haggai would make reference to the glory that belonged to it (Hag. 2:3).

The glory to which the prophet is referring would have been readily apparent to anyone who viewed Solomon's temple. Everything about it, its glimmering gold and shining bronze, testified to the glory of the God for whom it was built.

If Solomon's temple shouted, 'Glory!', how much more should the lives of Christians, who are his living temples and make up his church! (1 Cor. 3:16; 6:19-20; 2 Cor. 6:16). The apostle Paul calls upon believers to 'do all to the glory of God' (1 Cor. 10:31). And the apostle Peter tells us that God has made us his own 'special people' so that we may 'proclaim the praises' of the one who has called us 'out of darkness into his marvellous light' (1 Peter 2:9).

The temple says, 'Holy'

The glorious God whom the temple honoured is also a holy God. The very fact that the sanctuary was called 'the Holy Place' and the inner sanctuary 'the Most Holy Place' indicates his holiness. The fact that the high priest wore a plate with these words, 'HOLINESS TO THE LORD' (Exod. 28:36), indicates the same. That heavy curtain hanging there between the Holy Place and the Most Holy Place gave silent but mute testimony to the holiness of God. He is so holy that he cannot be approached by sinful men apart from atonement being made for their sins.

When Isaiah went into the temple on the occasion of Uzziah's death, he saw the Lord 'high and lifted up', and surrounded by seraphim who cried to one another:

Holy, holy, holy is the LORD of hosts;
The whole earth is full of his glory!

(Isa. 6:3).

We should note that the church of Christ is by her holiness of life to give testimony to the holiness of her God. Paul says the Lord Jesus 'gave himself' for the church 'that he might sanctify and cleanse her with the washing of water by the word, that he might present her to himself a glorious church, not having spot or wrinkle or any such thing, but that she should be holy and without blemish' (Eph. 5:25-27).

The apostle Peter issued this resounding call to holiness: '… but as he who called you is holy, you also be holy in all your conduct, because it is written, "Be holy, for I am holy" ' (1 Peter 1:15-16).

The temple says, 'Christ'

It cannot be stressed too strongly that Solomon's temple was designed by God himself to portray in advance the redeeming work of the Lord Jesus Christ. This connection is plainly set forth by the author of Hebrews. He tells his readers that Christ himself is both the sacrificing priest and the sacrifice offered by the priest. As the high priest entered the Most Holy Place once a year to make atonement for the sins of his people, so Christ entered 'the Most Holy Place once for all, having obtained eternal redemption' (Heb. 9:12). A little later he adds: 'For Christ has not entered the holy places made with hands, which are copies of the true, but into heaven itself, now to appear in the presence of God for us…' (Heb. 9:24).

Here is a clarion call to the modern-day church. As Solomon's temple testified to Christ, so the church is called to give testimony to Christ. This is her constant and unceasing obligation, her high and exhilarating privilege and her solemn duty for which she must give account. But one could easily get the impression that the church's task is something quite different. How little there is of Christ in many churches today! There is much about family living, managing finances, handling conflict and building self-esteem. There is much about living the 'victorious' Christian life, about tapping into God's power and getting him to do for us what we want done. There is much about mastering leadership principles. But there is little of Christ. It is terrible to have to admit this, but it is none the less true that it is possible for unbelievers to frequent services, even in evangelical churches, and hear virtually nothing at all about the glorious redeeming work of Christ. May God help each evangelical pastor to step into his pulpit with the request the Greeks made to Philip pounding and surging in his heart and mind: 'Sir, we wish to see Jesus' (John 12:20-21). Our congregations may not be saying this, but it will certainly help us keep on target if we picture them saying it. And if we will hold Christ faithfully before our hearers, we have reason to hope that by the grace of God this will indeed be their cry.

A temple temptation (6:11-13)

At some point during the seven years of construction work on the temple, the Lord spoke to Solomon. The central theme of the Lord's message was obedience. Solomon was to **'walk'** in the Lord's **'statutes'**; that is, to govern his life in accordance with the directions of the Lord. He was to **'execute'** the Lord's **'judgements'**; that is, to govern the nation according to God's laws. He was also to **'keep'** all God's **'commandments'** and **'walk in them'**. He was not to practise a convenient selectivity in regard to the commandments of God, but was rather to scrupulously and consciously adhere to all.

After emphasizing the importance of obedience, the Lord proceeded to reiterate his promise to perpetuate the throne of David. In one sense this promise was unconditional. God would perpetuate the throne of David in and through his Son, the Lord Jesus Christ. And he has done this apart from human

obedience. Nothing can, or ever will, thwart God's exaltation
of his Son.

In another sense, however — that of the throne of David
being 'visibly operative in every generation'[7] — the promise
to David was conditional. In other words, Solomon could only
expect succeeding generations to see a visible reign of one of
David's descendants if he and his successors obeyed the laws
of God.

We might say there were two tracks to God's promise of
the perpetuation of David's throne. One track is Christ's reign.
When he came to this earth, he was of the house and lineage
of David. He is David's greater Son and his kingdom will never
fail. The second track is David's other sons. They came to his
throne one after the other and, while some of them followed
the Lord, most did not. Their failure to do so brought an end
to the line of David as far as the visible success of his throne
was concerned.

We have only to look over a few centuries of time to see
how utterly serious God was about this matter of obedience.
He was not just 'bluffing' when he emphasized it to Solomon.
Solomon ultimately proved to be unfaithful to God's laws and
brought division upon his kingdom. Many of his successors
failed in the same way, as did their citizens, and the nation was
carried into captivity.

We have all seen parents who continually threaten to punish the disobedience of their children but never do, and we
may be inclined to think God is one of these parents, but he is
not. While he is always patient with his people and gives them
opportunity to repent, he will not put up with their disobedience for ever. In time he will make it abundantly plain that,
while we are often nonchalant and casual about the matter of
obedience, he never is.

We can well surmise that all of this came as a needed cor-
rective. The beauty and glory of the temple would pose to

Solomon and the people of Israel a serious temptation —
namely, to make the temple itself the focus, rather than the
Lord for whom it was being built. We need only travel a few
generations forward in time, to the days of the prophet Jeremiah, to see that this is indeed what took place. At that time
the people of Judah thought that the mere presence of the
temple assured them of God's favour. Meanwhile they gave
no thought at all to obeying his commands (Jer. 7:1-15).

The temptation to make the temple an end instead of a means
to a much larger end, worship of the true God, did not perish
with Solomon. Let us, therefore, heed the Lord's word about
the importance of obedience and not think mere religious activity is sufficient in and of itself. Just as God required obedience of Solomon, he requires obedience of his children today.
His demand has not been withdrawn, abrogated or annulled.

7.
A special day

Please read 1 Kings 8:1-13

There are ordinary days, and there are special days. We have here a day of days. It was such a grand day that many probably looked back upon it as the great highlight of their lives. On this day Solomon's beautiful temple, completed and furnished, was dedicated to the Lord.

This dedication day consisted of the following:

the moving of the ark and the tent of meeting (8:1-13);
Solomon's speech (8:14-21);
Solomon's prayer of dedication (8:22-53);
Solomon's blessing upon the people (8:54-61);
Solomon's feast of dedication (8:62-64).

And the day of dedication was then followed by several more days of joyous celebration and feasting (8:65-66).

We might be inclined, as we read the account of the dedication, to wonder what all the fuss was about. What made this day so very special and remarkable? The verses we are considering in this chapter enable us to provide answers to that question.

When it was scheduled

First, we must say it was a special day because of the timing of
it. We are told that the dedication was held **'at the feast in
the month of Ethanim, which is the seventh month'** (8:2).

Many have found it puzzling that Solomon selected this
time for the dedication in view of the fact that the temple had
been completed eleven months earlier (6:38; 8:2). Some have
suggested that the delay was necessary in order for all the
proper arrangements to be made, but it is doubtful that even
so elaborate an occasion would require this period of time. It
is more likely that Solomon selected this particular date because of its immense spiritual significance.

The feast 'in the month of Ethanim' was the Feast of Tabernacles (also known as the Feast of Booths or the Feast of
Ingathering). This event, the last of the yearly festivals, was
not only a harvest feast, but also a commemoration of the time
when Israel's forefathers moved into permanent dwellings in
the land of Canaan after years of living in temporary booths in
the wilderness (Deut. 12:8-11).

The Feast of Tabernacles was also significant because God
had demanded that the people of Israel renew their covenant
with him every seven years during the feast (Deut. 31:10-11).
R. D. Patterson writes, 'It is surely true that Solomon had in
his heart and mind the thought of covenant renewal, a personal and national rededication to God. It is not the ritual that
is emphasized but the outpouring of Solomon's heart to God.
What could have been merely a ritual dedication is transformed
into a genuine expression of praise and desire to serve the Lord.'[1]

What was carried into the temple

We must also say this day of dedication was special by virtue
of what was carried into the temple. Verse 4 says, **'Then they**

brought up the ark of the LORD**, the tabernacle of meeting, and all the holy furnishings that were in the tabernacle. The priests and the Levites brought them up.'**

The tabernacle of meeting

The tabernacle of meeting was the portable tent that was originally set up under Moses. At this particular time it was stationed
in Gibeon. It was designed to be Israel's worship centre until a
permanent temple was built, and now that its purpose had been
realized, it was stored in the new temple along with all its
furnishings. Because new, larger furnishings had been made to
replace those of the tabernacle, the latter could be stored.

The ark of the covenant

The most important of all the items transported to the new
temple was the ark of the covenant. David had moved it from
the house of Obed-Edom to the city of Jerusalem (2 Sam.
6:1-15), and now the priests moved it to the temple.

The ark was to be borne by the priests on long poles and
placed behind the thick veil in the Most Holy Place of the
temple where the atonement was made. The poles were to be
left in place (8:8). The purpose of allowing these poles to pro-
trude has caused considerable conjecture. Some think they
served to guide the high priest as he entered the darkness of
the Most Holy Place. Others think they served as a reminder
of the years that Israel bore the ark in the wilderness. Still
others suggest that they provided proof that the ark was there.

Whatever we conclude about those poles, it is evident that
the ark was the centrepiece of God's covenant with Israel. It
consisted of a box with a mercy-seat above it and cherubim on
each side with their wings outstretched over the box. All was
overlaid with gold. (The fact that there is no mention of Aaron's
rod and the pot of manna, which were originally laid alongside

the ark, indicates that these items had been lost). Inside the box were the tables of stone on which God had written the Ten Commandments.

The ark of the covenant was not just a quaint relic that the Israelites invented. It was a visible representation of the presence of God among his people through atonement of their sins by the shedding of blood.

The Ten Commandments inside the ark represented God's holy character and God's demand for his people to be holy. How few understand this these days! God's holy nature means that he cannot be ambivalent towards our sins. Because he is holy, he is indignant towards our sins. He cannot merely turn away from our sins and pretend that they are not there. The commandments of God make it plain that we must be holy, even as he is holy, before we can ever enjoy his presence in this life and before we can ever enter into his presence in eternity. These commandments describe for us the holiness that God demands. Scripture clearly shows that holiness is not just a matter of obeying these commandments in an external sort of way. God requires holiness in our desires as well as in our actions (Ps. 51:6; Matt. 22:37; Rom. 7:7,22). In addition to these things, the Lord prescribed eternal death for those who failed to keep his commandments.

As the Israelites of old reflected upon God's demands, they were filled with despair. What hope was there for people who had broken God's laws and stood under his sentence of eternal wrath? The ark of God gave the answer to that piercing question.

It is interesting that the mercy-seat on top of the ark was exactly the same width as the box containing the law. That mercy-seat was the place where the blood of atonement was sprinkled by the high priest on the annual Day of Atonement. This indicated that the blood of atonement perfectly satisfied the demands of God's law.

It is also striking that the cherubim were turned towards each other, each one looking down at the mercy seat. The cherubim are the highest of the angels. Because they are associated with the throne of God in Scripture, we can understand them to represent God himself. The fact that the cherubim on the ark looked down at the mercy-seat where the blood was sprinkled by the priest takes us to the heart of the meaning of the atonement. The cherubim, representing God, did not see the law and its demands because it was inside the box which was covered by the mercy-seat where the blood fell. When the high priest of Israel went into the Most Holy Place and sprinkled the blood of the sacrifice on the mercy-seat, it indicated that the demand of God's law for the death of the sinner had been satisfied. The blood of the mercy-seat covered the demand of the law. A. W. Pink writes, 'Suppose an Ark with no Mercy-seat: the Law would then be uncovered: there would be nothing to hush its thunderings, nothing to arrest the execution of its righteous sentence.'[2] Thank God for the mercy-seat!

The ark as a picture of the cross

Those who think that the Old Testament is the account of God vainly searching for a plan of salvation would do well to look at the ark of God. It was a glorious anticipation of the death of the Lord Jesus Christ on the cross. The apostle Paul says God the Father 'set forth' Christ as a 'propitiation' (Rom. 3:25). The Greek word translated 'propitiation' in this verse is translated as 'mercy-seat' in Hebrews 9:5. By his death on the cross, the Lord Jesus Christ became our mercy-seat.

To 'propitiate' means to 'appease or placate wrath or anger'. We have a tendency to think of Christ's death on the cross in terms of what it provided for us, that is, forgiveness of our sins and right standing before God. How seldom is it understood that the cross was also intended to do something for God! God's holy character is such that he is deeply insulted and offended by our sins. It is such that he is compelled to judge sin. He must carry out the sentence that he himself has pronounced upon the sinner, that is, eternal death. Only through the execution of that sentence can God's wrath against sin be placated or satisfied. If that sentence were not executed God would not be just.

There are only two ways for this sentence to be carried out. Either the sinner himself must bear the sentence, or someone must bear it in his place. The good news of the gospel is that God placated his wrath against his people by pouring it out on his Son, their substitute.

On the cross Jesus fulfilled what the types of the Old Testament could only anticipate and portray. There Jesus was both the high priest who offered the sacrifice and the sacrifice itself. He offered himself to God as the sacrifice for sinners. Drawing on the imagery of the Old Testament, we can say that the Lord Jesus sprinkled his blood on the mercy-seat of heaven (Heb. 9:1-28), and now all those for whom he died, God's elect, have nothing to fear from the law that demanded their condemnation. The blood of Christ fulfils that demand. On the cross he bore the wrath of God in the stead of his people, and they can now join the apostle Paul in saying, 'There is therefore now no condemnation to those who are in Christ Jesus...' (Rom. 8:1).

By his death on the cross Jesus completely and eternally satisfied both God's justice and mercy. Justice was satisfied because on the cross Jesus received the full measure of God's wrath against sinners. And mercy was also satisfied because, since Jesus took God's wrath on behalf of the believing sinner, there is no wrath left for that sinner to endure. Justice only demands that the penalty of sin be paid once and, if Jesus has paid it, there is nothing left for the one who is in Jesus to pay. Every Christian can, therefore, triumphantly sing with Elvina M. Hall:

Jesus paid it all,
All to him I owe;
Sin had left a crimson stain,
He washed it white as snow.

What came down into the temple

Finally, the dedication day was special because of what came down into the temple. After the ark was properly placed in the temple, a thick cloud so filled the temple that the priests were forced to stop their work (8:10-11).

This was not the first time such a cloud appeared. It appeared at Mt Sinai after the people of Israel were miraculously delivered from their bondage in Egypt (Exod. 24:15-17), and it appeared again when the tabernacle was completed (Exod. 40:34-38). On each of these occasions the cloud served as a visible manifestation of the presence of God. More particularly, it was a manifestation of the presence of his grace. For God to condescend to dwell among sinful people was gracious beyond description.

God's grace in no way, however, negates his glory. While the cloud testified to the presence of his grace, it was still a cloud, and much of God's glory remained hidden (8:12).

We sorely need to be reminded of the immensity of our God's glory. Howard F. Vos writes, 'Contemporary Christianity with its "buddy, buddy" approach to God has largely forgotten the sovereign glory and holiness of God, so that being a

Christian often seems to make little difference in the way we live.'[3]

All of this points us again to the Lord Jesus Christ. Never was the presence of God's grace more evident than it was in the life and ministry of Christ. But while occasional glimpses of his glory were seen (John 1:14), much of it remained hidden.

There is coming a day, however, when all that beclouds and obscures Christ will finally be removed, and all who know him as Lord and Saviour will then see the fulness of his glory. On that day they will marvel as never before at the grace that sent him to dwell with us and to provide eternal salvation for us.

8.
'Blessed be the Lord ...'

Please read 1 Kings 8:14-21,54-61

The lion's share of 1 Kings 8 is taken up with the spoken words of Solomon. He first addresses the Lord (8:12-13). He then turns to speak to those who had assembled for the dedication of the temple (8:14-21). He then speaks again to the Lord in a long prayer of enormous beauty and majesty (8:22-53). And he wraps it all up by once again addressing the assembly (8:54-61). In this chapter we consider his two messages to the vast assembly (8:14-21,54-61).

Solomon begins each of these two messages with the phrase: **'Blessed be the Lord'** (8:15,56). This tells us that he was occupied with the Lord and what he had done. Solomon could have brought attention to himself. He could have ordered the day's events in such a way that praise was heaped upon himself for his careful planning, shrewd negotiating and wise leading. Or he could have heaped praise upon the people for all they had done to make the temple a reality. But Solomon knew the truth of the matter. The praise properly belonged to the Lord. All that he and his people had done was the result of the Lord's graciously working in them and enabling them.

It may seem to some to be quite needless to call attention to Solomon's emphasis on the Lord on this occasion, but the truth is that we have come to a day in which we sadly need this emphasis. It is amazing how little of God there is in many services that are purportedly held to bring honour to his name. The worshippers themselves are much in evidence. Their needs, desires and experiences hold centre stage, while God's glorious person and his saving gospel are left in the background. Even many of the so-called 'praise' choruses seem to give more attention to the ones doing the praising than to the God who is supposedly being praised. Solomon did not make this mistake, and we would do well to learn from him.

A promising God who keeps his promises

Solomon's first address

One aspect of the praise Solomon offered on this day may be summarized in this way: God is a promising God who keeps his promises (8:14-21,56).

Solomon began his first address to the people by reminding them that God had spoken to his father and predecessor, David (8:15). David had desired to build the temple, but while commending him for the desire (8:18), the Lord had forbidden him to do so (8:19). God's purpose for David was to secure peace for the kingdom. That having been accomplished, David's own son would succeed him and build the temple.

During his final days, David saw the first of these promises fulfilled as his son Solomon came to the throne. The fulfilment of the second promise he did not live to see, but it came true none the less. Solomon spoke of God's faithfulness to these two promises in these words: **'So the LORD has fulfilled his word which he spoke; and I have filled the position of my father David, and sit on the throne of Israel, as the Lord promised; and I have built a temple for the name of the LORD God of Israel'** (8:20).

Solomon's second address

Solomon also struck this note of praise for God's faithfulness in his second address, reaching this time all the way back to Moses, who received instructions for building the portable tabernacle that preceded the temple. Solomon said, **'Blessed be the LORD, who has given rest to his people Israel, according to all that he promised. There has not failed one word of all his good promise, which he promised through his servant Moses'** (8:56).

This is quite a startling statement. We generally consider someone to be faithful if he keeps most of his promises and commitments. But Solomon celebrated, not a God who is generally faithful, but rather one who is perfectly faithful. He says, 'There has not failed one word of all his good promise...' Not one word! That is faithfulness with a vengeance!

Solomon was not allowing himself to get carried away by the emotion of the moment. The faithfulness of God to his promises was writ large in the history of the nation of Israel. God had promised to deliver her from bondage in Egypt, and he did. God had promised to drive their enemies from the land of Canaan and settle them there, and he did. God promised to bless them as they lived in obedience to his commands, and he did. God had promised to give them a king after his own heart, and he did so in David. And, as we have noted, God had promised David that his son would succeed him and build the temple, and we find that son dedicating the temple in this chapter.

This is nothing less than God being faithful to the covenant he had established with the people of Israel. In this covenant God pledged himself to bless the obedience of his people and to curse their disobedience (Deut. 28:1-68). The dedication of the temple gave this generation of Israelites the opportunity to rejoice in the blessings God had promised to bestow upon his faithful people. Their descendants would see the other side of the matter. They would turn from the Lord to worship idols, and God, in perfect covenant faithfulness, would mete out the curses he had promised, including drought and eventual captivity.

The book of 1 Kings is, then, a book about Deuteronomy as it details both the covenant blessings and curses. It looks at God's people through the lens of Deuteronomy. This perspective is evident again in the passage we consider in our next chapter, when Solomon offers certain detailed requests to the Lord in his dedication for the temple.

God's ongoing faithfulness

This represents only a sample of the promises that God had fulfilled. And there were yet more to come. This same God who had fulfilled these promises had promised to provide a Redeemer. The fulfilment of that promise was still centuries away, but it was fulfilled there in tiny Bethlehem when Jesus was born. And the redemption God had promised through his Son was fulfilled when Jesus died on the cross and arose from the grave.

All of this has great meaning for us. The very God who made and kept promises to Israel of old has made promises to us as well. He has promised forgiveness of sins to all who cast themselves completely on the atoning sacrifice of his Son. God can be trusted to keep that promise. He has promised that his Son will some day return to take all those who know him to share his glory in heaven. God can be counted on to keep that promise. God has promised to give his people strength and grace while they wait for that glorious day in heaven. The God who has demonstrated his faithfulness time and again can be depended upon to be faithful to this promise as well.

A present God who keeps his people

Another aspect of the praise Solomon offered on this occasion is this: God is a present God who keeps his people (8:57-61).

Solomon was profoundly grateful for the blessings the Lord had bestowed in the past. Without God's blessings, there would have been no Israel, no Solomon and no temple. But Solomon was also keenly aware that the blessings of the past, staggering as they were, were not sufficient for that time. Therefore, after praising God for keeping his promises, Solomon turns to register his intense desire for the Lord to continue to bless his people.

A desire for obedience

First, he expressed his desire for the Lord's enabling grace in the matter of obedience (8:57-58,61). Solomon knew that the Lord desires obedience from his people, that he delights to bestow his blessings upon people who conduct their lives according to his **'ways'**, **'commandments'**, **'statutes'** and **'judgements'** (8:58).

Furthermore, Solomon realized that God's people are not capable in and of themselves of maintaining the obedience the Lord demands. It was necessary, therefore, for the Lord himself not to forsake them (8:57) so that he could **'incline'** their **'hearts'** to himself (8:58).

In expressing this desire, Solomon was in no way seeking to absolve himself and his people of responsibility. His final words on this grand occasion make that clear: **'Let your heart therefore be loyal to the LORD our God, to walk in his statutes and keep his commandments, as at this day'** (8:61).

Perhaps someone will be inclined to see a contradiction here. Does the obedience of the child of God hinge on God or on the believer? Is it the product of God's enabling the believer, or is it the product of the believer's diligent efforts? Is it the result of God's inclining the heart of the believer to obedience, or the result of the believer's inclining his own heart in that direction? It is both. The obedience of the believer is at one and the same time the result of God's working in him and that believer's diligently walking with God.

This is made plain by the apostle Paul in these words: 'Therefore, my beloved, as you have always obeyed, not as in my presence only, but now much more in my absence, work out your own salvation with fear and trembling; for it is God who works in you both to will and to do for his good pleasure' (Phil. 2:12-13).

Obedience is, therefore, the result of the Lord's enabling and his people's response to his enabling. How tragic that Solomon himself, after speaking such eloquent and moving words, was eventually to fail to respond to the Lord's enabling grace! After urging his people to let their hearts be loyal to the Lord (8:61), Solomon failed to keep his own heart loyal and went after idols.

A desire for truth to be displayed

Secondly, Solomon also expressed his desire for the Lord's enabling grace in the area of displaying his truth (8:59-60).

The nation of Israel was like no other. She had a special **'cause'** (8:59). God had called her into a covenant relationship with himself that she might show forth his glory. She was called to live in such a way **'that all the peoples of the earth may know that the LORD is God; there is no other'** (8:60). This was a cause that was far too demanding for Solomon and his people. It required the day-by-day presence of God, remembering his people and manifesting his grace in their midst.

The two desires Solomon expressed in his closing words — enabling grace to obey and enabling grace to extend his kingdom — were not a matter of the king seeking to top off a special day with a poetic flourish. Those desires flowed from a heart that was not only aware of the premium God placed on these things, but also of how incapable the people of God are of producing them.

Much has changed since Solomon spoke these words on this occasion. But one thing has not changed: God still demands that his people obey him and seek to extend his kingdom. And the God who demands these things still supplies his people day by day with grace to produce them. Blessed be the Lord!

9.
With Solomon in the school of prayer

Please read 1 Kings 8:22-53

These verses lay before us the matter of prayer. Here we have the long prayer Solomon prayed at the dedication of the temple. This prayer gives each child of God much cause for self-examination. In addition to relating Solomon's prayer on this significant occasion, this passage compels us to ask ourselves if we know anything about this type of praying.

A convert from Hawaii shared this assessment of Christian praying with some American seminary students: 'Before the missionaries came to Hawaii, my people used to sit outside their temple for a long time meditating and preparing themselves before entering. Then they would virtually creep to the altar to offer their petition and afterward would again sit a long time outside, this time to "breathe life" into their prayers. The Christians, when they came, just got up, uttered a few sentences, said "Amen", and were done. For that reason my people called them *haolis*, "without breath", or those who failed to breathe life into their prayers.'[1] We need not endorse all these Hawaiians did to breathe life into their prayers in order to understand the importance of having life in our prayers. Solomon's prayer had life in it, and it shows us how to have life in our prayers.

Warm-hearted adoration

Solomon's is a prayer of warm-hearted adoration of the Lord
(8:23). The king comes into the presence of the Lord, not in a
sterile, mechanical way, but with a real spirit of worship and
praise. He celebrates the uniqueness of God. There is no one
like God. Men have designated many things as gods through
the running centuries, but the God to whom Solomon prays
does not have to be designated or selected as God. He is the
eternal one who made all things and who rules and reigns over
them.

This incomparable God has, in grace that boggles the mind,
stooped down to his sinful creatures. He is a God of covenant
mercy. The nation over which Solomon ruled was testimony
to that covenant mercy. God had long ago called the nation
into a special covenant relationship with himself, a relationship that required the people to walk before him **'with all
their hearts'** (8:23).

The temple Solomon and the people of Israel were dedicating on this occasion gave eloquent testimony to the covenant mercy of God. The God who cannot be contained by
heaven itself had condescended, in a sense, to dwell in Solomon's little temple (8:13,27,29). How could such a thing be?
Paul House answers: 'God is lofty, holy, and mysterious, yet
approachable and personal at the same time. The temple will
serve as the physical symbol of these divine realities. Here the
unapproachable Lord becomes approachable and ready to help
those who worship, sacrifice, and pray.'[2]

Solomon's adoration of God abounds with meaning for us.
It tells us that great praying is born in great awareness of the
greatness of God. Such awareness is produced by feasting on
the Word of God. The key to effective praying, then, is not to
rush into the presence of God to present our petitions, but
rather to remind ourselves of the majesty and glory of the one
we are approaching.

A profound sense of unworthiness and deep humility

Solomon's prayer challenges us at another point as well. It is a prayer that reflects a profound sense of unworthiness and deep humility (8:27-30).

Solomon did not, as it were, casually stroll into the presence of God as his equal. Far from it! He was overwhelmed, as we have noted, by the thought that the God of heaven would condescend to dwell among his people (8:27).

The king knew he and the people of Israel were not worthy of even the least of God's blessings. Four times in these verses he refers to himself as God's **'servant'** (twice in verse 28 and once each in verses 29 and 30). A master is not under obligation to his servant. A servant is not in a position to make demands. All the servant can do is recognize his unworthiness and cast himself upon the mercy of his master. This is the position Solomon takes in these verses. He asks as a servant for the mercy of the Lord upon himself and his people.

One does not hear much about humility these days, but the fact that it is not popular does not make it optional. After urging his readers to be 'clothed with humility', the apostle Peter writes, 'Therefore humble yourselves under the mighty hand of God, that he may exalt you in due time...' (1 Peter 5:5-6).

Faith in God's revealed Word

A final point at which Solomon's prayer challenges us is this: it is a prayer that reflects faith in God's revealed Word. This feature emerges in two ways. First, Solomon specifically asks the Lord to keep his promises (8:26). Secondly, he offers seven detailed petitions that were based on the promises of God.

A request for God to keep his promises

Solomon's specific request for God to keep his promises arose
from his keen awareness of the promise-keeping nature of God.
He was particularly aware of the fulfilment of God's promises
to his father David. The temple itself was the fulfilment of one
of those promises (8:19-21), as was Solomon's reign (8:20,25).

After celebrating the fulfilment of these promises, Solomon makes this request: **'And now I pray, O God of Israel,
let your word come true...'** (8:26). Specifically, Solomon
was asking God to grant perpetuity to the kingdom of Israel
and to sons of David upon her throne.

Seven detailed requests

Solomon's seven detailed requests also teach us to pray on
the basis of God's promises. It is important to note that Solomon did not just make these requests up, or pick them out of
the air. They were all informed by Scripture. Five of these
seven petitions ask God to relieve his people of various calamities they would bring upon themselves through sin. The
Lord had long ago warned the nation of Israel about disobedience and had promised to visit upon their disobedience the
very calamities Solomon mentions in his prayer (Lev. 26; Deut.
28-30).

Each of these requests is signalled by the formula **'when
... then'** (8:31-32,33-34,35-36,37-39,41-43,44-45,46-49).
The last of the seven features two usages of the 'when ...
then' formula (8:46-47,48-49).

The first of these requests deals with vindication for
the innocent in cases of inter-personal disputes in which
dishonest people swore false oaths (8:31-32).

The second asks for God's forgiveness for sin that caused his people to be defeated in battle (8:33-34).

The third asks for forgiveness of the sin that caused drought (8:35-36).

The fourth asked for forgiveness when God's people, knowing the 'plague' of their own hearts (8:38), turned to God after experiencing famine, pestilence or other plagues (8:37-40).

The fifth moves away from the calamities created by the sinfulness of God's people to a much happier eventuality, namely, the turning to God of those from other countries (8:41-43). This would be the inevitable result of these people's hearing what God had done in Israel. Solomon looks forward to this result and asks God to answer the prayer of these foreigners.

The sixth petition considers soldiers who do not have access to the temple because of their engagement in warfare in foreign lands (8:44-45). Solomon asks God to hear their prayers and maintain their cause.

The final petition takes up yet another calamity caused by the sin of the people, that is, captivity in a foreign land (8:46-53). Solomon prays that the Lord would forgive his people and show compassion towards them (8:50) **'when they come to themselves'** (8:47), repent and return to God with all their hearts. This request also rests upon God's promise that he would indeed show mercy to his people upon their confession of sin (Lev. 26:40-42).

It seems to many to be senseless and needless to pray on the basis of God's promises. If God has promised to do something, and he is always faithful to his promises, why ask him to keep his promises?

The answer is that God is the Father of his people and he delights, as any good father does, in his children coming to him and asking him for what he has promised. It gives him pleasure to hear the prayers of his children and to answer those prayers according to his unsearchable wisdom and his unfailing promises.

A picture of Christ

We urgently need the lessons Solomon's prayer has to teach. This is good, solid praying — praying that adores God, that flows from a humble heart and that clings tenaciously to the promises of God. While it is good and beneficial to look to Solomon's prayer for guidance and instruction on our own praying, we must go a step further. We must also look at his prayer as a picture of the current and ongoing work of our Saviour, the Lord Jesus Christ.

Solomon has often been regarded as a type of Christ in many ways. His wisdom and justice are only faint glimmers of the wisdom and justice of Christ. The glory of his kingdom must certainly be taken as a foretaste, or anticipation, of the glory of Christ's kingdom. But at no point in his life did Solomon more typify the Lord Jesus Christ than in this prayer. In this prayer Solomon interceded for his people. In like manner, the Lord Jesus Christ makes intercession for his people (Rom. 8:34). He is in the presence of the Father as our Advocate (1 John 2:1), and just as Solomon prayed for God to forgive the sins of his people, so Christ asks the Father to forgive his people.

The knowledge of Christ's intercessory work is in and of itself enough to encourage us to give ourselves to the same adoring, humble, trustful prayer that Solomon exemplified on this occasion.

10.
A multitude of sacrifices; an abundance of joy

Please read 1 Kings 8:62-66

These verses bring us to the end of the activities and ceremonies surrounding the dedication of Solomon's temple. There had never been anything in the life of the nation that could compare to this dedication. It brought Israelites from as far north as Hamath, on the one hand, and as far south as the border of Egypt, on the other (8:65). The dedication would by itself have been a great attraction, but this event had an even greater appeal because it was immediately followed by the Feast of Tabernacles, which was observed each year in the month of Ethanim, the seventh month (8:2, cf. Lev. 23:34).

The keynote in this concluding description of these days is abundance, and this abundance was primarily manifested in two ways: in the sacrifices offered by the worshippers and in the joy which they felt. Such abundance was fitting. It is the nature of God to bless his people abundantly, a truth captured and expressed by David:

> They are abundantly satisfied with the fulness of your house.
> And you give them drink from the river of your pleasures.
> For with you is the fountain of life;
> In your light we see light
>
> (Ps. 36:8-9).

Those who have been 'abundantly satisfied' with the goodness of God cannot help but desire to give abundant expression to that satisfaction.

The multitude of sacrifices

We first notice that Solomon and the people offered sacrifices in staggering numbers. The number was so large that **'the middle of the court that was in front of the house of the Lord'** had to be consecrated for that purpose (8:64). 22,000 bulls and 120,000 sheep were offered as peace, or fellowship, offerings (8:63). There were also burnt offerings and grain offerings (8:64).

The nature of Solomon's offerings

The nature of these offerings should be noted. The *peace offering* was a shared offering. A bull, cow, lamb or goat could be used. Part of the animal was offered up to God. Part of it (the breast and right thigh) was taken by the priest and part was eaten by the worshipper as a meal of celebration (Lev. 7:11-21,28-36). Because of its shared nature, this sacrifice represented fellowship between God and man.

The *burnt offering* represented complete dedication to God. A young bull, lamb, goat, turtledove, or young pigeon could be used, but the animal had to be a perfect and complete specimen (Lev. 1:3-17).

The *grain offering* was a bloodless offering from the harvest of the land. It had to be finely ground to remove all coarseness. It accompanied all burnt offerings and signified thanksgiving to God (Lev. 2:1-16).

These sacrifices undoubtedly seem to many to be nothing more than the bizarre attempt of an ancient and benighted people to curry favour with their God, and to have absolutely no significance or meaning for us. Such a view is far removed from the truth. Israel's sacrificial system was not only designed and instituted by God himself, but was done for the express purpose of pointing to the death of the Lord Jesus Christ on the cross.

The offerings as anticipations of Christ

How beautifully Christ is prefigured in the sacrifices of Solomon and his people! He is there in the burnt offerings, the grain offerings and the peace offerings.

The *burnt offerings* typified Christ in that he completely dedicated himself to God and was completely consumed by the fire of God's judgement there on the cross of Calvary.

The *grain offerings* typified his humanity. As the offerings were without coarseness and leaven, so our Lord was without any taint of evil (1 Peter 1:19).

The *peace offerings* represented the peace that comes between the holy God and sinners as a result of Christ's totally offering up his perfect humanity to God on the cross.

This brings us to the very core of the Christian message. Man as God created him enjoyed perfect fellowship with God, but through sin that fellowship was disrupted and broken. As far as the sinner is concerned, dealing with his sin should be a very simple thing. He thinks God should have responded to Adam's sin by shrugging and saying, 'Let's just forget about it.' But God's nature will not allow him to do that. He is holy, and his holiness requires him to take sin seriously and punish it. Before fellowship between God and the sinner could be restored, therefore, something had to be done about his sin. God's holiness demanded that the penalty for sin be paid, and the penalty for sin is eternal death.

Here is the glory of the Christian gospel. The Bible tells us that the very God who d mands that the penalty of sin be paid has himself paid the penalty. The Second Person of the Trinity took unto himself our humanity, and in that humanity went to the cross. There he received an eternity's worth of wrath for sinners. God's justice only requires that the penalty for sin be paid once, and since Christ paid for it there is no penalty left for all those who cast themselves totally and unreservedly upon his redeeming death. And since Christ has paid for their sin and taken it out of the way, fellowship with God is restored.

The apostle Paul celebrates this glorious truth in these words: 'Therefore, having been justified by faith, we have peace with God through our Lord Jesus Christ...' (Rom. 5:1). Paul further exults that he and his fellow-Christians were once enemies of God, but have now been 'reconciled to God through the death of his Son' (Rom. 5:10).

The offerings as pictures of the Christian's walk with God

The offerings of Solomon and his people have relevance for us on another level as well — that is, as pictures of the Christian's walk with God. As the burnt offerings reflected total devotion to God, so all who are saved are called to present themselves as 'living sacrifices' who are totally dedicated to the Lord (Rom. 12:1).

As the grain offerings reflected the thanksgiving of those who offered them, so we are called to 'continually offer the sacrifice of praise to God, that is, the fruit of our lips, giving thanks to his name' (Heb. 13:15).

And as the peace offerings reflected the worshippers' enjoyment of fellowship with God, so we are called to offer the sacrifice of obedience to God by walking according to his commandments. While sin cannot destroy our relationship with God, or completely negate our fellowship, it can disrupt and hinder it. We must, therefore, 'walk in the light as he is in the light' (1 John 1:7).

The abundance of joy

This truth puts us in a position to note the second area of abundance in these verses: the abundance of joy with which the Israelites finally left the days of dedication.

Their departure occurred on **'the eighth day'** (8:66). This is somewhat confusing because of the reference to fourteen days in the previous verse. The key to resolving this difficulty is to keep in mind that two feasts, each lasting seven days, are described in this eighth chapter. The first is the feast of dedication and the second is the Feast of Tabernacles. Of course, on this special occasion, they effectively blended into one gigantic celebration of fourteen days. When the author tells us the people departed on the eighth day, he is referring to the day after the second feast, the Feast of Tabernacles, was complete.

More important than the time when the people departed is the manner in which they departed. We are told that when Solomon sent the people away, **'They blessed the king, and went to their tents joyful and glad of heart for all the good that the LORD had done for his servant David, and for Israel his people'** (8:66).

These people left with the keen awareness that all they had witnessed in the past few days was testimony to the goodness of God. It showed that God had kept the promises that he had made to David (2 Sam. 7:12-16) and that he had poured out his blessings upon Israel. As they reflected upon the goodness of God, they could not help but be 'joyful and glad of heart'.

It is easy enough to see the goodness of God to the Israelites. Their nation was at peace and enjoying prosperity. Their king was a wise administrator. They now had a beautiful temple. What we often fail to see is that God has been enormously and immensely good to all who know him. He has rescued us from the just condemnation of our sin. He has reconciled us to himself and made us part of his family. He has given us the Holy Spirit to guide, strengthen and comfort us. He has given us title to eternal life. He has done it all through his Son, Jesus Christ.

How profoundly grateful we should be for the goodness of God! But one gets the impression that those who profess to know the Lord are not especially known for being 'joyful and glad of heart'. We often go to our services and come away from them, not as if we had just tasted of the Lord's goodness, but rather as if we had been occupied with a tiresome chore. We often find complaints spilling from our lips while praise withers and dies. This may seem to be mere quibbling to some, but it is not. Unbelievers make up their minds about the genuineness of Christianity by what they see in us. And they are quick to spot drooping, whining Christians and to conclude that Christianity must have very little to offer.

So the word is 'abundance'. Let's reflect on the abundant nature of Christ's sacrifice for us, and let's give ourselves to abundantly sacrificing to him. As we do so, let us make sure we have an abundant supply of joy and gladness of heart. Who knows what might result from such things?

11.
Manifold blessings

Please read 1 Kings 9:1-28; 10:11-29

Perhaps no words are more frequently used by Christians than 'blessing', 'blessed' and 'bless'. It is not hard to see why this should be the case. These words crop up constantly in Scripture. The word 'bless' appears 132 times, the word 'blessed' 285 times and the word 'blessing' seventy times.

To be blessed, or to receive a blessing, means to be in a state of happiness because of some good the Lord has bestowed. In the early part of his reign, Solomon and his people were in a state of happiness because the Lord had bestowed good upon them. Their enjoyment of such blessings gave testimony to the Lord's faithfulness to his promises.

The option of blessing or cursing was constantly before the people of Israel. This was powerfully demonstrated when Moses placed half of the assembled tribes of Israel on Mt Gerizim and the other half on Mt Ebal. The former pronounced God's blessing on those who obeyed his laws, while the latter pronounced his curse on those who disobeyed (Deut. 27:11 - 28:68). We might say Solomon and his people had been living on Mt Gerizim; that is, they had been living in obedience to the Lord and had been receiving his blessings. Little did they realize that the shadow of Mt Ebal was hovering over them. They moved from the mount of blessing to the mount of cursing when they moved from obedience to disobedience.

In this portion of 1 Kings, however, Solomon and his people are still on Mt Gerizim. In the passages which form the subject of this chapter the author focuses our attention on two of God's blessings on Solomon at this time: God blesses Solomon by appearing to him (9:1-9) and by giving him even more success (9:10-28; 10:11-29).

God appears to Solomon

The first occasion

Consider first the blessing God bestowed upon Solomon by appearing to him. It would have been a signal blessing indeed had the Lord only appeared to Solomon on one occasion. Many great men of faith in the Scriptures were never granted a special appearance at all, but here the Lord appears to Solomon a second time.

The first appearance, at Gibeon, early in Solomon's reign, consisted of the Lord's graciously offering to give Solomon whatever he asked. Solomon responded to this grace by asking God for an understanding heart and discernment in judging the people (3:5-9). God had honoured that request, and the kingdom had arrived at a place of unprecedented prosperity. The marvellous temple had been built, as had Solomon's own house. The nation was at peace. Israel was the envy of all the nations.

The second occasion

Such prosperity can be very dangerous. It has a way of lulling to sleep and creating a false sense of security. Through this second appearance, the Lord gave Solomon some words of warning.

Indeed, the Lord first assured Solomon that his prayer regarding the temple had been heard, and that the Lord would be present there in a special way (9:3). But from that point of reassurance the Lord moved quickly to emphasize the matter of obedience, even to the point where the rest of his message was occupied with it (9:4-9).

This call to obedience consisted of both a positive and negative thrust. The former emphasized the blessing that obedience to God would bring (9:5). The latter emphasized the calamities that disobedience would bring about (9:6-9).

The blessing consisted of Solomon's sons continuing to reign over Israel (9:5). The Lord's promise to David of permanence for his throne is, of course, fulfilled in and through the Lord Jesus Christ. That promise of permanence did not necessarily entail an unbroken line of David's sons reigning. That could have been the case had the sons of David obeyed the Lord's commands, but, as we shall see, they failed to do so.

The kings of the nation were not the only ones to fail in this matter of obedience. The people joined with them in this failure. These failures, as the Lord made clear to Solomon in this appearance, would lead to some very negative and disastrous results. In addition to the line of David's sons on the throne being broken, the nation itself would be **'cut off'** from her land, would become an object of ridicule among the nations, and the temple, so beautiful and brilliant now, would be so ruined that all those who passed by would be astonished (9:7-8).

We know that these were not mere empty threats. All of these dire predictions came true to the very last detail. The people of God were indeed carried away from their land into captivity. Their beautiful temple was indeed destroyed. And the people of God were indeed ridiculed by the surrounding nations.

The testimony of disobedient people

It was all so unnecessary. If Solomon, his sons and the people of Israel had only heeded the message of the Lord, they could have continued to enjoy the blessing of the Lord. But they forfeited those blessings and endured fearful calamities because of their stubborn refusal to obey.

They leave on the pages of Scripture mute but eloquent testimony to several truths. Here is testimony to the premium God places on this matter of obedience. We are very impressed with emotional experiences in religion, but God is far more impressed with our obedience than with our ecstasies.

Here also is testimony to what constitutes obedience. It is not a matter of our deciding for ourselves what pleases the Lord and acting accordingly. No, obedience is determined by an objective standard. It is not a matter of how we compare with others, or how we measure up to the latest opinion poll. God has clearly laid out in his Word what he desires of us, and obedience is a matter of adhering to that Word. It is not only a matter of outward conformity to these guidelines but also a matter of inward conformity. We are to **'walk'** before the Lord **'in integrity of heart'** (9:4).

We also find here a clear word about how the Lord regards idolatry. We like to think that all sins are equal in the sight of God, but the truth is that he regards some sins as being particularly heinous. Nothing stirs his displeasure so much as sustained idolatry. That occurs when his people draw away from him and give to any other thing the allegiance and the devotion that belong to God, and God alone, and when they refuse to heed all warnings regarding this sin but persist in it.

This passage also demonstrates the influence God's people have for good or ill upon others. The Lord's people are always on display. They do not live in a vacuum. Unbelievers are aware when God's people are walking close to him and enjoying his blessings. And they are aware when God's people stray from him and experience his chastisement. They are ever eager to seize the latter as proof that there really is nothing to this matter of knowing God and serving him.

God grants success to Solomon

One would have thought that this second appearance of the Lord would have been more than enough to persuade Solomon to keep walking in the pathway of duty, but the Lord went even further by heaping upon him even more success (9:10 - 10:29).

These successes were many and very impressive. Border towns that Solomon originally offered to Hiram of Tyre in payment for building materials were rejected by Hiram and, presumably, rebuilt and settled by Israelites.[1]

Additional building projects were undertaken and completed (9:15-16,24-26). Wilderness areas were developed for military purposes (9:17-19). Israel's long-time enemies were suppressed and put to use (9:20-23). A seaside city was developed into a trade centre, into which gold and other goods poured in great abundance (9:26-28; 10:11).

In addition to these things, Solomon's wisdom and glory had become so widely known that the Queen of Sheba came to gain first-hand knowledge of them (10:1-13). She was not alone. The author tells us, **'All the earth sought the presence of Solomon to hear his wisdom, which God had put in his heart'** (10:24). And as they came they brought even more goods to enrich Solomon even further (10:25).

The last half of chapter 10 relates the blessing of God in terms of the enormous wealth that was Solomon's (10:14-23,

26-29). Gold, silver, exotic animals, horses and chariots —
Solomon possessed them all in abundance. Verse 23 summar-
izes the riches of Solomon in these words: **'So King Solomon surpassed all the kings of the earth in riches and wisdom.'** It was all from the hand of the Lord. Early in Solomon's reign the Lord had promised to give him riches and
honour so there would not be anyone like him among the kings
of his time (3:13).

But along with these unsurpassed blessings came God's
unrelenting demand for Solomon's obedience, a demand he
sadly failed to meet, as we shall see. No one has ever been
more blessed than Solomon, and in the light of the blessings
bestowed upon him, we have to say no one has failed more
dismally than he.

In many ways, Solomon, as we have noted, prefigured the
greatest of all kings, the Lord Jesus Christ. But let it be noted
that Solomon was definitely not a type of Christ on this matter
of obedience. Solomon failed, but Jesus did not. He kept the
laws of God in every respect. Because of his obedience he
was sinless, and because he was sinless he had no sin of his
own for which to pay. He could, therefore, pay for the sins of
others. This was one of the essential ingredients in his being
able to save. Of course, he also had to be fully God so he
could fully bear God's wrath against the sins of all the elect.
Through him alone, his people have eternal salvation. How
grateful we should be that he could truthfully say, 'A greater
than Solomon is here'! (Matt. 12:42).

12.
The Queen of Sheba

Please read 1 Kings 10:1-13

When the news of Solomon's wisdom reached the Queen of Sheba, her curiosity was more than a little stirred. The report she heard connected the glory and wisdom of Solomon with **'the name of the LORD'** (10:1). As far as she was concerned, such a report could not be ignored. She would go to Israel, meet this king, see his glory and learn about this God.

Her arrival in Jerusalem must have been a very impressive sight as she came with **'a very great retinue'** that included many gifts for Solomon (10:2).

Her visit to Solomon proved to be everything she expected and more. His wisdom, which allowed him to answer all her questions (10:3), his abounding prosperity and the orderly conduct of his affairs (10:4-5) made a profound impression upon her. Having witnessed it all, she told Solomon that the report she had heard of him, while true, was only partial. She said, **'... indeed the half was not told me'** (10:7). She then proceeded to pronounce all Solomon's servants as being **'happy'** (10:8), to bless the Lord concerning whom Solomon had instructed her (10:9) and to bestow gifts upon Solomon in staggering abundance (10:10), gifts to which Solomon responded **'according to the royal generosity'** (10:13).

This account goes far beyond one monarch visiting another. It is full of spiritual lessons for us. In fact, we are entitled to look upon the visit of the queen as a picture of the sinner coming to the Lord Jesus Christ. This is legitimate because the Lord Jesus himself used the visit of the queen to convey to the Pharisees what constitutes a true response to himself (Matt. 12:42).

There are three major parallels between the queen coming to Solomon and the sinner coming to Christ.

Reported fame

First, there is the parallel of reported fame. The Queen of Sheba came to Solomon after hearing reports of his fame (10:1), and the sinner comes to Christ after hearing reports of him and what he has done.

These reports of Christ may come in various ways, but the primary way is through the preaching of the gospel. Here is cause for each preacher to examine himself. It is the preacher's task to make the fame of Christ known. It is to be feared that there is much to lament here. One gets the impression that many pulpits are devoted to publicizing the fame of the preacher's wit and ability to entertain, or the fame of his ability to help his hearers cope with life's problems. But few seem to be devoted to publicizing the fame of Christ.

This dreadful lack should cause each preacher to weigh carefully the apostle Paul's series of piercing questions: 'How then shall they call on him in whom they have not believed? And how shall they believe in him of whom they have not heard? And how shall they hear without a preacher? And how shall they preach unless they are sent?' (Rom. 10:14-15).

The preacher is to include several things in the report he gives of Christ. He is the Second Person of the Trinity who has always existed with God the Father and God the Spirit. He joined with the Father and the Spirit in the planning of redemption before the world began. In the fulness of time he left the throne of his glory and, without diminishing or lessening his eternal deity, took unto himself our humanity, so that he was fully God and fully man at one and the same time. He took unto himself our humanity, not in the normal way, but through being born of a virgin. As a man, he was subject, as all men are, to the laws of God, but whereas all others have failed to obey, he did not. His was a seamless life in which he perfectly loved God and perfectly adhered to his commandments.

Having lived a perfect life, the Lord Jesus Christ went to the cross upon which he died. He was not there as a mere hapless victim who could not help but die. He freely, deliberately and willingly went to that cross. Those who crucified him thought he was there because he could not help but be. In one sense they were correct. He could not help but be there, but what held him there was not weakness, as they supposed, but rather strength: the strength of his love for God the Father and his love for sinners. On that cross he died no ordinary death, but received in his own person the wrath of God for sinners.

After he died, he was buried, but he did not stay in the grave. On the third day he arose, as he had promised, and forty days later ascended to the Father in heaven. He is now at the right hand of the Father to make intercession for all those who come to God by him.

That brings us to another parallel between the Queen of Sheba and the sinner, that is, the parallel of response.

Eager response

On hearing the report of Solomon's fame, the Queen of Sheba determined that she would go to him with her questions. Some suggest that she was sceptical about the report she had heard and went to Solomon to prove to herself that the report was wrong, that she went to confound him with riddles he could not possibly answer.

Alexander Maclaren responds to this suggestion in these telling words: 'The journey was too toilsome, the gifts too large, the accent of conviction in her subsequent words too grave for that. She was a seeker after truth, and probably after God, and had known the torture of the eternal questions which rise in the mind, and, once having risen, leave no rest till they are answered.'[1]

Once in Solomon's presence, the queen **'spoke with him about all that was in her heart'** (10:2), and Solomon answered **'all her questions'** (10:3). In fact, the queen found that **'There was nothing so difficult for the king that he could not explain it to her'** (10:3). What a model there is here for the unbeliever! The Queen of Sheba arises, as it were, from her generation to say to each unbeliever, 'You have heard a marvellous report about Christ. Now go to him! Take all those questions about God and eternity that so vex and torment you, and ask him.' Those who bring such questions to Christ will find answers and their torment will vanish and be replaced by the peace of God.

What are these tormenting questions about God and eternity that Christ so perfectly answers? Here are some suggested by Charles Spurgeon:

How can a man be just with God?
How can God be just, and yet the justifier of the un-
     godly?
How can God, who sees all things, no longer see any sin
     in believers?
How can a man's life be in heaven while he still lives on
     earth?[2]

These and many other hard questions are answered by the Lord Jesus Christ. And he himself is the answer! But the one who comes to Christ to seek answers must come seriously and sincerely. Christ is not in the business of granting satisfaction to those who come to him only to propound riddles that are designed to disprove Christianity. Those who are concerned with how many angels can dance on the head of a pin will, unless they repent, learn only how many demons dance in hell!

But those who come labouring and heavy laden with the questions of how sin can be forgiven and heaven can be attained, and speak to Christ about these things from their hearts, will find a sympathetic hearing and a satisfying answer.

Those who hear the report about Christ and refuse to go to him will find that they themselves will some day meet this Queen of Sheba. She will 'rise up in the judgement' and 'condemn' them because 'She came from the ends of the earth to hear the wisdom of Solomon,' and the Lord Jesus Christ is far greater than he (Matt. 12:42).

Lavish praise

That brings us to yet another parallel, the parallel of praise. After receiving sufficient answers for her questions, the Queen of Sheba was filled with astonishment and praise. The report she had heard did not begin to approximate to the reality she had experienced (10:7). As she reflected on that reality, she realized how privileged the servants of Solomon were to serve him and to be so near him that they could benefit from his wisdom (10:8).

Similar thoughts fill the heads of all those who come to faith in Christ. They find that the joy of knowing salvation through him far exceeds the grandest report they ever heard

about him, and they realize for the first time what they have
been missing and how blessed are those who came to Christ
before them and have for some time been occupied with serving him.

To those who have not yet come to that faith I say, learn
from the Queen of Sheba. You have heard the report about
Christ. Don't be satisfied just to hear it. Come now to Christ
and receive what he offers. If you will do that, you will have to
say with the Queen of Sheba, 'Indeed the half was not told
me' (10:7).

13.
The turning-point

Please read 1 Kings 11:1-13

Solomon's was the glorious reign with the ghastly end. The glory part of it came as he walked in obedience to the Lord and received from the Lord unprecedented wisdom and glory. The ghastly part of it came when he turned from the Lord to embrace idols. The downfall of a great person is always sad, and the greater the person, the greater the sadness. There has never been a sadder downfall than the one recorded in this passage. Here the great Solomon turns from God.

What an enigma Solomon was! He was at one and the same time the wisest of men and the most foolish of men. His wisdom lay in God. His foolishness lay in forsaking the very God who had given him that wisdom. Solomon was the most foolish wise man who ever lived — the wisest fool!

None of us will ever begin to approach the wisdom and glory of Solomon, but we can certainly duplicate his foolishness. We can turn from the God who has so immensely and consistently blessed us to worship false gods. We can do so, as Solomon did, after many, many years of faithful service to the Lord. Because this matter of turning from God is an ever-present and real danger, we would do well to look closely at these verses and enquire concerning the cause, the character and the consequences of Solomon's turning.

The causes of Solomon's idolatry

What caused Solomon to turn from the Lord? These verses
identify two major causes. First, there was what we might call
the external factor, that is, his foreign wives (11:1-2). These
women came from nations that served other gods and they
persuaded Solomon to make provisions for their idols.

We all have our weaknesses, and we tend to think they will
be our downfall. Sometimes, however, it is the areas where
we are strongest that ruin us. This may very well have been
the case with Solomon. His foreign wives may have appealed
to his great wisdom to persuade him to do what they wanted.
S. G. DeGraaf suggests that they flattered him by constantly
reminding him that he was the most enlightened ruler of all
times and encouraged him on the basis of that to appreciate
the progress and contributions of other nations.[1] If they took
this line of reasoning, they would most certainly have proceeded to point out that the progress of these nations could in
no way be attributed to the God of Israel because these nations
worshipped other gods. One as enlightened as Solomon would
surely permit his wives to continue to worship the gods that
had done so much for their nations! They would not deny
Solomon's God, but neither did they want him to deny their
gods!

If all this has a familiar ring to it, it is because the appeal to
'enlightened tolerance' is still very much with us. How often
Christians hear this appeal! Critics and sceptics hear us talk
about sinful human nature and they are amused. No one be-
lieves that any more! They hear us talk about the bloody death
of Christ on the cross as the only possible means of salvation,
and they can barely believe that anyone should be so totally
lacking in sophistication. How dare anyone suggest that his
way is the correct way and other ways are mistaken! How

bigoted and intolerant! The critics and sceptics learn of our belief in judgement to come and they are again astonished. The mere suggestion that some will be separated for ever from God stirs their wrath. How could anyone be so benighted as to hold such a position?

And many professing Christians, aware of how revolting their beliefs are to the majority and not wanting to be considered out of step, begin to adjust and modify and reduce them until they are holding a message that bears precious little resemblance to the historic Christian faith.

Appeals to his enlightenment would not have been effective with Solomon had it not been for *an internal factor*, that is, the condition of his heart (11:4). It is very easy to lay all the blame for Solomon's downfall at the feet of his wives, but that would be like Adam and Eve blaming the serpent for their sin. Yes, the wives put significant pressure on Solomon, but the real problem was that Solomon had allowed his heart to drift from the Lord!

How deceptive and treacherous are our hearts! The seeds of rebellion and backsliding always reside in them, and they will produce a sizeable crop if we are not watchful. It is more than a little ironic that Solomon himself had already written these perceptive words: 'Keep your heart with all diligence, for out of it spring the issues of life' (Prov. 4:23). Solomon failed to heed his own advice. He did not guard his heart, and a bumper crop of rebellion and disobedience sprang up.

We are told that Solomon **'clung'** to his wives **'in love'** (11:2). If he had only clung to the Lord in love, all would have been well, but the clinging that should have been reserved for the Lord alone was directed towards those who were adamantly opposed to the Lord.

The character of Solomon's idolatry

This brings us to consider something of the character of Solomon's turning from the Lord. It was a most startling and audacious thing. We must characterize it in this way because the Lord had been so good to Solomon. He had not only given this man wisdom and glory that were the envy of all, but had actually appeared twice to him (11:9, cf. 3:5-15; 9:1-9).

God had also been clear with Solomon. Solomon had the law of Moses before he ever ascended to the throne, and that law was strikingly plain in regard to the king taking foreign wives (Deut. 17:17) and in regard to any Israelite going after other gods (Exod. 20:3; Deut. 28:14; 30:17-18). This was more than sufficient, but God had also spoken explicitly to Solomon about the danger of idolatry (11:10, cf. 9:6-9).

But the goodness of the Lord and the clarity of his commands notwithstanding, Solomon listened to his wives and turned to idols, and did so in a most disgusting and shocking way. He **'went after'** the Sidonian goddess Ashtoreth, the goddess of sex, and the Ammonite god Milcom (11:5). He even went so far as to build high places for the Moabite god Chemosh and the Ammonite god Molech (11:7). This is especially shocking because human sacrifices were often included in the worship of these gods.

S. G. DeGraaf conveys something of the enormity of Solomon's actions in these words: 'He allowed altars for the idols to be erected near Jerusalem — on the holy ground which was to be cleansed of the Canaanites so that only the Lord would be served there. The idols were worshipped right in front of the Lord, who revealed the presence of His grace in the temple!'[2]

The consequences of Solomon's idolatry

All that Solomon did was known to the Lord, and the Lord was not neutral about it. Some time after Solomon began to walk this path, the Lord spoke to him regarding the consequences of it (11:11-13). The proud, glorious kingdom of Solomon was to experience profound humiliation. It was to be violently torn from the house of Solomon and given to one of Solomon's servants (11:11).

God fulfilled his warning to the letter. After Solomon died, the kingdom was divided into two parts. Ten tribes retained the name Israel and were ruled by Jeroboam, the head of Solomon's slave-labour force. Two tribes, Judah and Benjamin, became known as the kingdom of Judah and continued to be ruled by the descendants of Solomon.

That Solomon's house retained a part of the kingdom is a testimony to the grace of God. God does not forget to be gracious even in the midst of his judgements. Judgement is his 'unusual' work (Isa. 28:21). He never delights in it and always tempers it with mercy.

But the traces of God's grace in his judgement should not be taken to mean those judgements will not be severe. Solomon's kingdom was about to learn just how severe judgement can be. Division was looming before them, and a few centuries later both kingdoms would find themselves in captivity in foreign lands. The glory of Solomon's kingdom was about to vanish, and it was all due to his turning from the Lord and embracing idols.

Ashtoreth, Milcom, Chemosh and Molech are gone, but the threat of idolatry remains. Pleasure, possessions and prestige constantly beckon us to come and serve them, as does every easy-going religion that discards the very heart of the historic Christian faith in order to offer what pleases.

We may follow these gods and other false gods for a time without experiencing dire consequences. We may even assure ourselves that such consequences will never come, that we are getting away with our idolatry. Sinners always take the delays of God to mean judgement is not coming. But God will not always delay, and judgement will come, and when it comes we shall rue the day when we first thought we could turn from the Lord with impunity.

14.
A lasting lesson from ancient adversaries

Please read 1 Kings 11:14-43

The apostle Paul wrote, 'Do not be deceived, God is not mocked; for whatever a man sows, that he will also reap' (Gal. 6:7). The apostle was not announcing a new law when he wrote those words. The law of sowing and reaping has been in place from the beginning of human history. It cannot be set aside or nullified. King Solomon knew about this law but chose to ignore it and, in doing so, brought heartache to himself and to his nation.

Solomon's refusal to heed this law is a most astonishing thing. For years he reaped positive benefits as he remained faithful to the Lord. That alone should have been sufficient to keep him walking in the path of obedience to the Lord, but as we noted in the last chapter, he turned from the Lord. Even though the Lord had been nothing but good to him, Solomon strayed from him and went after other gods (11:4).

In this passage the author details for us some of the evil consequences that attended Solomon's sin.

Three adversaries

These consequences primarily came to Solomon in the form of three adversaries: Hadad (11:14-22), Rezon (11:23-25) and Jeroboam (11:26-40).

Hadad was an Edomite who, having survived David's severe slaughter of 18,000 Edomite males (2 Sam. 8:13-14; 1 Chr. 18:12-13), found refuge in Egypt until he was ready to return to his homeland and launch some sort of resistance against Solomon.

Rezon also escaped one of David's attacks, this one against Zobah, and set himself on a course of opposition to David's successor, Solomon. His opposition was effective enough for him to seize control of Damascus.

While these two men were in place from the beginning of Solomon's reign, their strength and influence were apparently so small that they were of no concern to Solomon and he could legitimately say, 'There is neither adversary nor evil occurrence' (5:4). All of that changed abruptly with Solomon's idolatry as the Lord made the efforts of these men far more effective in the latter years of his reign.

While Hadad and Rezon were worrisome to Solomon, they did not pose as serious a threat as *Jeroboam* the Ephraimite. An **'industrious'** man of **'valour'**, Jeroboam had caught the eye of Solomon, who made him head of his labour force from the tribes of Ephraim and Manasseh (11:28). This happy beginning was not to continue. Jeroboam soon became disenchanted with the king, **'rebelled'** against him (11:26) and eventually split the kingdom.

What was the source of his disenchantment? The text gives us the impression that it was fuelled by the message of Ahijah the prophet. The appearance of Ahijah marks a major transition. Ahijah is the first prophet to appear in 1 Kings. (Although Nathan the prophet appeared briefly in the first chapter, it was as a friend to David and his family rather than in his role as a prophet.) The remaining chapters of 1 Kings will report a steady succession of prophets. The prophets would become an essential element in the nation's life because of the steady slide of the people into idolatry. Their continuing presence also gives testimony to the faithfulness of God to his people and his patience with them.

Ahijah confronted Jeroboam one day as the latter was leaving Jerusalem and escorted him to a field where they could be alone. There the prophet suddenly took the new garment he was wearing, tore it into twelve pieces and told Jeroboam to take ten of them (11:29-30).

Jeroboam did not have to wait long for an explanation of this act. The ten pieces of cloth represented the ten tribes over which the Lord was going to make him ruler. The other two tribes — later referred to as one (11:36) because Benjamin had for all practical purposes become absorbed in Judah — would remain under the rule of the house of David. In this way the Lord would continue to honour his covenant with David (11:34).

Another indication of the Lord's faithfulness to his covenant with David was his promise that the division would not take place until after Solomon was dead. The implication is that the Lord had promised David that Solomon would continue to reign over the entire kingdom as long as he lived (11:34; cf. 2 Sam. 7:15).

The answer to our question about the source of Jeroboam's disenchantment with Solomon would seem, then, to be this: Jeroboam took Ahijah's prophecy as a licence to force the issue. Ahijah was telling Jeroboam what God was going to do for him. All Jeroboam had to do was to go about his business and wait for the Lord to fulfil his promise. He was called to do as David had done when Saul was king. Although David had been anointed to be king, he did not take matters into his own hands and seek to force Saul from the throne. He was content to wait upon the Lord to bring him to the throne. But Jeroboam, unwilling to take this approach, started a rebellion against Solomon, a rebellion that was unsuccessful and ended in his having to flee to Egypt.

The lasting lesson

We have looked at the three adversaries that God raised up to trouble Solomon, but if we leave the matter there, we have done nothing more than delve into history. We must look beyond mere history to the spiritual reality that is just as present today as it was in Solomon's time — that is, the presence of adversity in the lives of God's children.

All God's children know what it is to face adversity of some sort. Sometimes the adversity comes upon us, as it did in Solomon's case, because of our disobedience to the Lord. In other words, the Lord can, and does, send chastisement upon his children, even as he did with Solomon.

Christians these days find this to be a most distasteful subject, so much so that many consider it to be out of keeping with what the Bible says about God as a loving Father. No matter how unpleasant it is, we cannot dismiss it because it is clearly taught in the Word of God. In addition to teaching the reality of chastisement, the author of Hebrews goes so far as to assert that it is not a contradiction of God's love, but rather a manifestation of it. He writes:

> My son, do not despise the chastening of the LORD,
> Nor be discouraged when you are rebuked by him;
> For whom the LORD loves he chastens,
> And scourges every son whom he receives
>
> (Heb. 12:5-6).

This author then proceeds to add: 'If you endure chastening, God deals with you as with sons; for what son is there whom a father does not chasten? But if you are without chastening, of which all have become partakers, then you are illegitimate and not sons' (Heb. 12:7-8).

This chastening of the Lord can take a good many forms. It can come in the form of the Lord's withholding blessings from us. It can come in the form of his sending calamity upon us. It can even come in the form of a combination of the two. But whatever form it takes, its purpose is the same — that is, to correct the straying saint so that he will yield 'the peaceable fruit of righteousness' (Heb. 12:11).

Scripture does not explicitly say that Solomon came to his senses and repented before he died, but if we assume that he was indeed a child of God (and it is unthinkable to assume that he was not), we may safely conclude that he came to lament the folly of his idolatry and to repent of it, a repentance that evidently did not leave him time to purge the idolatry from the land.

We are wise if we learn from Solomon. No matter how many blessings we have enjoyed and no matter how long we have walked with the Lord, we are never exempt from God's call to obedience. We must ever be aware of the high premium God places on it, and we must ever be on guard to avoid it. We must especially guard our hearts against the sin of idolatry, that sin in which we give to something else the allegiance and devotion that belong to God alone.

We easily fall into the trap of thinking of idolatry as a sin of the ancient past. The truth is that it is the great sin of the church today. How lightly and easily the people of God put personal pleasure above the house of God and the work of God! It may seem for a while that we are able to do this without incurring any great loss. But if we continue to do it, we invite God to withhold his blessings and to send adversity upon us. Continued invitations to God's chastisement will most certainly ensure that it will some day come to visit.

While it is true that God can and does chastise his children by sending adversity their way, it must also be said that not all

adversity comes upon us because of disobedience. Some comes
to us because of our righteousness. We have to look no further than Jesus himself for an example of this. No one experienced more adversity than he, but that adversity was due, not
to his sin — for he had none — but rather to his complete
allegiance to God. We shall never be as completely devoted to
God as he was, but to the degree that we are devoted to God,
we can expect to encounter the hostility of Satan and his people.

15.
Human folly and
divine sovereignty

Please read 1 Kings 12:1-24

This chapter brings us to one of the most important events in the entire Old Testament. Here the nation of Israel, so wondrously blessed by God, is torn into two parts.

The first verse alerts us to the presence of deep trouble in the nation. The ten northern tribes of Rehoboam's kingdom had evidently made it clear that they did not regard him as their king simply because he had ascended to the throne in Jerusalem. They wanted to meet and to deliberate with him and, if all went well, accept him as their king.

The representatives of these tribes were not even willing to go to Jerusalem, the religious and political centre of the nation, to meet with Rehoboam. They beckoned him, as one would a servant, to come to Shechem, a place associated with renewal (Gen. 35:1-4; Josh. 24:1,14-28). Perhaps they were hoping it would prove to be the place of renewal of the bond between themselves and the house of David.

No portion of Scripture is at one and the same time more depressing and cheering than the one before us. The depressing effect comes from its sustained emphasis on human folly. The cheering effect comes from its calm assurance that God is at work in the midst of human folly to achieve his purpose.

Human folly

Folly enjoyed a field day at Shechem when Rehoboam jour-
neyed there. That folly is evident in the following ways: the
absence of any spiritual emphasis, Rehoboam's harsh response
to the request of the northern tribes and those tribes' aban-
donment of the house of David. We can refer to these as the
folly of all, the folly of Rehoboam and the folly of the northern
tribes.

The folly of all

Ronald S. Wallace takes us to the heart of this folly with this
insightful observation: 'As we read of the gathering at Shechem
to appoint their future king we are meant to note the secular-
ity that now prevailed within the nation's life. The issues before them were critical and decisive for their future. Yet no
priest was invited, no prayer was offered, no reference at all
was made to God and his will...'[1]

This was out of keeping with what the nation had done on
many previous occasions when issues of great importance were
being decided (Josh. 24:1; 1 Sam. 10:19; 2 Sam. 5:3; 2 Chr.
29:20-21). On those occasions they were first concerned 'to
ensure the presence and blessing of God'.[2]

True religion had so deteriorated in the nation that no one
— not Rehoboam, Jeroboam, Rehoboam's advisers, or the
elders of the northern tribes — even suggested that they begin
their deliberations by seeking God. No one at Shechem even
mentioned the Lord. This is shocking in the light of the fact
that God's covenant nation was discussing the one who was
to rule with the knowledge that it was God, and not himself,
who was the nation's true King.

The folly of Rehoboam

The folly of failing to seek God created other follies. When Rehoboam arrived in Shechem he found Jeroboam on hand as the spokesman for Israel (12:2-3). Jeroboam made it clear that the ten northern tribes were not satisfied merely to have Rehoboam come to Shechem. Before they would accept him as their king they must have his firm assurance that he would lighten the heavy load of taxation and forced labour that his father Solomon had placed upon them (12:4). If that demand were met, they would be willing to serve him.

The counsel of Rehoboam's older advisers was very sound. If Rehoboam wanted the people of Israel to serve him for ever, it was necessary for him to be their servant on the issue they had raised with him (12:6-7).

Rehoboam's younger advisers took precisely the opposite tack. If the people there at Shechem succeeded in dictating to Rehoboam on this matter, they thought he would be for ever kowtowing to them. He must, therefore, show decisively that he was the boss.

Rehoboam accepted this advice and promised that he would add to the burden his father had placed on the people. Solomon, he said, had whipped them with whips, but he would use 'scorpions', that is, whips with sharp pieces of metal attached (12:14).

The folly of the northern tribes

If Rehoboam thought Jeroboam and the northern tribes would be cowered and intimidated by his tough talk, he was in for a rude surprise. The people responded by saying:

What share have we in David?
We have no inheritance in the son of Jesse.

To your tents, O Israel!
Now, see to your own house, O David!

(12:16).

If we look only at the politics of this situation, we might find ourselves siding with the northern tribes. Their request appears to have been very reasonable, and their pledge to give their support if their request was met seems to have been utterly sincere (12:4). The folly of their position lies in their ignoring the spiritual dimension of being connected with the house of David. The Lord had established a special covenant with David. He had promised a permanence for David's house that could be achieved only by the coming of the Messiah (2 Sam. 7:16). With this in mind, S. G. DeGraaf lays before us the enormity of Israel's turning away from Rehoboam: 'They knew about the promise which had been given to David's house. Wilfully they rejected that promise and — with it — the Lord's covenant.'[3]

We should not let the fact that God had promised to divide the kingdom (11:31) persuade us that the northern tribes were free from folly in this situation. God can and does work through the foolish wickedness of men without approving of it. The division of the kingdom was at one and the same time God's judgement on the wickedness of Solomon and the result of the folly of men. We have a hard time reconciling how men can be responsible and God be sovereign, but the Bible assures us that both are true. There is no greater example of this than the death of Jesus on the cross, which was due both to the eternal plan of God and the wickedness of men (Acts 2:23).

Divine sovereignty

On the surface it may appear that the events of Shechem were nothing more than an example of the ill results of bad political judgement. But in the affairs of men there is always another level — the divine level.

This division was primarily due to the fact that the Lord ordained it. There can be no doubt about this. The author puts it bluntly: ' **... the turn of events was from the LORD...**' (12:15). The same truth was affirmed by the Lord himself in the message he delivered to Rehoboam through Shemaiah: **'This thing is from me'** (12:24).

Why did the Lord design and orchestrate the division of the very kingdom that he had so signally and continually blessed? It was because both Solomon and his subjects had turned from him to worship and serve idols (11:33).

The great, overarching theme of this passage is, then, the sovereignty of the God who controls all things. This God is not at a loss as to how to bring his purposes to pass. He is not at the mercy of kings and rulers. In fact, as Solomon himself observed:

> The king's heart is in the hand of the LORD.
> Like the rivers of water;
> He turns it wherever he wishes
>
> (Prov. 21:1).

The Lord is not sitting in heaven wringing his hands in dismay. He is not lamenting his inability to achieve his purposes because wicked men and women will not let him. He is not the author of their wickedness, but neither is he defeated by their wickedness. He can, and does, use the wickedness of men to bring glory to his name and to further his plans.

Because God is sovereign and in control, his word is true and utterly dependable. God does not make promises and then fret and worry over whether he will be able to keep them. He does not need men to make his promises come to pass, and men cannot keep his promises from coming to pass.

Through Ahijah the prophet the Lord promised Jeroboam that he would cause him to reign over ten tribes (11:31). But the Lord did not need Jeroboam to force the issue. In his own time, the Lord delivered those tribes to him just as he had promised.

Furthermore, the Lord was not in a panic while Rehoboam and the people of Israel were deliberating. The Lord didn't have to look on helplessly and say, 'I hope Rehoboam makes the right decision. If he doesn't, I won't be able to fulfil my promise.' The very Lord who had declared his intention to divide the kingdom worked through Rehoboam's counsellors to bring that division about.

All the Lord did to bring about the division of this kingdom serves as an example of his working to fulfil a much larger plan, namely, the plan to bring his Son, Jesus Christ, into this world to provide eternal salvation for believers. How hell plotted and schemed to prevent that! But all its schemes could not prevent Jesus from coming. Hell could not even delay his coming by a single moment. He came, according to the apostle Paul, in the fulness of time (Gal. 4:4); that is, at exactly the right time, the time marked out before the world began.

The same God who made promises regarding kings and kingdoms and regarding salvation through his Son has also made promises to us about what lies ahead. He has promised that this same Jesus will come again, receive his people unto himself and take them with him to share in his eternal glory.

Let all hell rage, that promise is going to be fulfilled. It does not matter how wolfish are the devil's wolves and how sheepish the Lord's sheep, the sovereign God is going to achieve everything he set out to achieve. With that knowledge in hand, those of us who know the Lord need not be filled with fear and anxiety. Our God is in control! It is ours, not to worry, but merely to trust and obey.

16.
Jeroboam's folly

Please read 1 Kings 12:25-33

Jeroboam came to the throne of Israel with a distinct promise from God. Through his prophet Ahijah the Lord spoke these words to Jeroboam: 'Then it shall be, if you heed all that I command you, walk in my ways, and do what is right in my sight, to keep my statutes and my commandments, as my servant David did, then I will be with you and build for you an enduring house, as I built for David, and will give Israel to you' (11:38).

Jeroboam had already seen the first part of the Lord's promise come true. The Lord had indeed given Israel to him. Rehoboam had come to Shechem expecting to become king of the whole nation and had left as the King of Judah, and Jeroboam had been crowned by the ten tribes of Israel (12:20).

It cannot be emphasized too strongly that all this had been promised by the Lord. Because the division of the kingdom had taken place just as the Lord promised, it should have been a very easy thing indeed for Jeroboam to trust the Lord's promise to give him an enduring house. That portion of the promise was just as clear as the part about the division of the kingdom. All Jeroboam had to do to receive this enduring house was to obey the commandments of the Lord (11:38). He had to do what Solomon had failed to do.

No one has ever come to a throne with his duty more plainly prescribed than Jeroboam. It was especially important for him to avoid the sin of idolatry. This was the sin that had provoked the Lord to divide Solomon's kingdom.

Jeroboam's fear (12:26-27)

With all this in place, we might find it rather startling to read these words: **'And Jeroboam said in his heart, "Now the kingdom may return to the house of David..."'** (12:26).

Specifically, Jeroboam was afraid that his people would continue to journey to the temple in Jerusalem to offer their sacrifices, and it would, therefore, only be a matter of time before they would kill him and give their allegiance to Rehoboam (12:27). Jeroboam's phrase, **'their lord, Rehoboam king of Judah'**, makes it appear that he considered his own reign to be illegitimate. This was a false conclusion. His reign was ordained of God, and the continuation of it hinged on obedience to God. But Jeroboam lacked faith. Although he had already realized one part of the promise, that he would rule over ten tribes, he doubted the other part, that his reign was secure as long as he obeyed God. Doubting that part of the promise, he did the very thing that was certain to bring his kingdom to an end — that is, disobey the commandments of the Lord.

Jeroboam's response (12:28-33)

Jeroboam could most certainly have sought out Ahijah and conveyed his fear about the future of his kingdom. If he had done so, he would undoubtedly have been reassured by the prophet. But Jeroboam rejected this course and turned to some of his political advisers. Bad advice had caused Rehoboam to adopt a foolish strategy (12:6-14), and now it causes Jeroboam to do the same. All turning from God and embracing what is false begins when we stop relying on what God has revealed in his Word and begin relying on our own wisdom. Jeroboam's reliance on human wisdom led him to construct a false religion and to defend it with a shameful rationale.

The false religion

Jeroboam's new religion consisted of two golden calves (12:28-29), shrines on the high places (12:31), a priesthood from among the people (12:31) and an annual feast (12:32).

The golden calves. Jeroboam did not think he was setting up a new religion. The golden calves, which were stationed at Bethel in the south (approximately eleven miles north of Jerusalem) and Dan in the northernmost part of the kingdom (12:29), were not intended to replace God, but rather to aid the worship of him. Jeroboam did, after all, connect these calves with Israel's deliverance from Egypt. That was, of course, a wonderful display of the power of God on behalf of his people. The calf, or bull, was a common symbol in those days for power, and Jeroboam, by constructing two calves, may have thought he was bringing double honour to God by focusing on his power.

But God is not honoured merely by our good intentions, or by what we in our wisdom conclude. He is honoured by our obedience to his Word.

Jeroboam's calves failed on a grand scale. First, they failed properly to honour God's power. His power, unlike the bull's, is without limit. Secondly, the calves failed because they focused on only part of the truth about God. God is powerful, but he is also just, holy, gracious, wise, faithful and eternal, omnipresent and omniscient. The calves, then, actually diminished the very one they were supposed to honour. Finally, these calves had the effect of blurring the line between the worship of God and the worship of Baal in that the calf was also used in the fertility religions of the Canaanites.

Jeroboam and his advisers should have known better. Centuries before, God had visited severe judgement upon Israel when Aaron constructed a golden calf for the people to worship (Exod. 32:1-35).

The shrines on the high places. In addition to the two national shrines at Bethel and Dan where the golden calves were stationed, Jeroboam set up local worship sites on various **'high places'** (12:31).

The priesthood. A religion has to have priests, and Jeroboam filled this need by opening the priesthood to any and all who wanted to serve (12:31). The tribe of Levi had been designated by God as the tribe from which the priests were to come, but the Levites were going about their duties in the temple in Jerusalem. Even if they had been available to Jeroboam, they would not have wanted anything to do with his new religion.

The annual feast. Jeroboam's religion was complete with his institution of a feast that would be held in Bethel a month before the Feast of Tabernacles in Jerusalem (12:32). By putting his feast in advance of the one in Jerusalem, Jeroboam hoped to dissuade his people from going there. The problem with this feast was the same as with all of Jeroboam's innovations. They were **'devised in his own heart'** (12:33), rather than being ordained of God.

With the addition of the feast, Jeroboam had his new religion in place. Paul House offers this summary of it:

The institutionalization of a non-Mosaic religion is now complete. A syncretistic mix of Yahwism and Baal-worship is in place. Northerners will have to make a special effort just to worship the Lord. Just as there are now two nations, two capitals, two governments, and two kings, there are also two religions. The major differences are as follows:

Judah	*Israel*
No images of God	Veneration of calves
Levitical priesthood	Multi-tribe priesthood
Central sanctuary	Local and regional sanctuaries
Separatist cult	Syncretistic cult[1]

The shameful rationale (12:28)

With his false religion in place, all that remained for Jeroboam to do was to sell it to his people. He did this by telling them that it was **'too much'** for them to continue to go to Jerusalem. The people did not seem to share Jeroboam's concern. Those in the southern part of his kingdom seem to have passed by the closest calf at Bethel so they could worship at the one in Dan. Convenience appears to be of concern only to those who are looking for a way to get around worshipping the true God. The point is, however, that Jeroboam considered convenience to be a sufficient basis for the people to make their religious choices.

It is good for churches to consider the convenience of worshippers in such matters as constructing buildings, providing parking and establishing starting times for services. But it is not good when churches move to the area of convenience those matters that God has declared to be essential and nonnegotiable. For example, attending public worship is not to be determined on the basis of whether it is convenient for us. It is commanded (Heb. 10:25).

Even more troubling is the current trend to downplay or remove those elements of the gospel that people find to be distasteful and inconvenient: the total depravity of man, the sovereignty of God, the blood atonement of Christ, the certainty of judgement. Many churches, out of the desire to grow in numbers, have already abandoned these scriptural truths and are declaring a message of easy Christianity, one that we may have by 'accepting' Jesus, or 'inviting' Jesus into our hearts, and one that is simply concerned to tell us how to cope with our busy and challenging lives.

In such a climate, we need frequently to remind ourselves of the warning of Paul about 'peddling' the Word of God (2 Cor. 2:17), that is, using it in such a way as to guarantee only positive results. Those who use the Word of God in this way seek to eliminate what Paul calls the 'aroma of death' (2 Cor. 2:16) from it. Little do they realize that in doing so they also eliminate the aroma of life. In other words, when we try to take out of the gospel those truths that offend, we end up taking out the very truths that can give spiritual life.

'The way of Jeroboam'

Jeroboam's religion represented such a complete break with God-ordained worship and such a pivotal juncture in the life of Israel that the author of 1 Kings adopts the phrase 'the way of Jeroboam' as convenient shorthand for characterizing the kings who were to succeed him (e.g. 15:26,34; 16:19,26).

Jeroboam joins Cain and Balaam, then, in having a 'way'. One takes the way of Cain (Jude 11) when one refuses to submit to God's way of salvation and depends rather on one's own works. One takes the way of Balaam (2 Peter 2:15) when one uses one's spiritual gifts for the purpose of securing material well-being. And one takes the way of Jeroboam when one turns a heedless ear to God's revealed truth and follows idolatrous innovations.

17.
A hard-hitting prophet and a hard-hearted king

Please read 1 Kings 13:1-10

Immediately after describing Jeroboam's plunge into idolatry, the author writes, **'And behold, a man of God went from Judah to Bethel by the word of the LORD'** (13:1).

With those words the author reminds us that God is not a helpless spectator of human events. He did not merely stand by wringing his hands in despair as Jeroboam created his false religion, but took action by sending a prophet from Judah to Bethel. Paul House rightly notes: 'God is fully sovereign in history, a fact that his sending of prophets to make predictions conveys...'[1]

The prophet confronts the king (13:1-6)

A threefold prophecy (13:1-3)

The prophet from Judah, unnamed by Scripture, takes his place as one who performed admirably. He met Jeroboam while the latter was burning incense on his idolatrous altar at Bethel (13:1). Ignoring the king, the prophet proceeded to cry out against the altar. His prophecy was startling and riveting. First, he predicted that a man named Josiah would spring from the house of David. Secondly, he declared that this Josiah would desecrate the altar by burning on it the bones of the priests who had used it (13:2). Thirdly, he said that, as a sign that the first two prophecies would come to pass, the altar would be split open and that its ashes would pour out (13:3).

The first two predictions of this amazingly detailed prophecy would require approximately three hundred years for fulfilment, but they came true to the letter. After the nation of Israel was carried into captivity by the Assyrians, one of David's descendants, Josiah by name, came to Bethel and burned the bones of the priests on the altar (2 Kings 23:16).

A hostile response (13:4-5)

Jeroboam did not wait to see if the third part of the prophecy, the altar splitting open, would come true. Instead he pointed towards the prophet and commanded his guards to arrest him. As he did so, he received a sign which the prophet had not announced. His hand withered, and he was not able to pull it back to his body. And then the sign which had been announced occurred as the altar split apart and its ashes poured out (13:5).

A gracious restoration (13:6)

The withering of his hand caused Jeroboam, for the only time recorded in Scripture, to be softened towards the things of God. He immediately moved from commanding the prophet's arrest to seeking his help. He asked the prophet to **'entreat the favour of the Lord'** so that his hand might be restored. The prophet did as the king asked, and the Lord graciously restored the king's hand.

The prophet rejects the king's invitation (13:7-10)

In the splitting apart of the altar and the withering and restoration of his hand, Jeroboam was given in quick succession three signs confirming the validity of the prophet's message and the enormity of his own sins. The proper response to all these things would have been a deep and sincere repentance before God and a cleansing of the land of the idolatry that he had introduced.

But while Jeroboam was impressed and even grateful, he was not changed. Instead of repenting, he invited the prophet to his home and promised him a reward (13:7). Many try to satisfy God's demand for repentance by offering some sort of religious activity that is less painful. They will not break with their sin, but they will make a donation to the church. They will not repent, but they will attend the services for a while.

The prophet categorically refused the king's invitation by revealing the instructions he had received from the Lord. He was neither to eat nor drink in Bethel and was to return to his homeland by another way (13:9). The prophet's instructions revealed the depth of the Lord's revulsion over Jeroboam's idolatry. For the prophet to eat and drink at Bethel would have been tantamount to his fellowshipping with the idolaters. Jeroboam's idolatry was so detestable to the Lord that the very path the prophet had walked to reach Bethel was, as it were, defiled and should not be walked again. The prophet's instructions may seem to us quaint and unnecessary, but they serve as lasting reminders of eternal truths: God's people are not only to refuse to fellowship with idols (1 Cor. 5:11) but are also to despise anything that entices or leads to idolatry.

At this point in his mission the prophet of Judah speaks forcefully to us about the importance for God's people of living on the basis of his revealed Word. That Word may have seemed outdated and outmoded as he stood there at Bethel amidst the trappings of Jeroboam's innovative and appealing religion, but the prophet functioned on the basis of it. The church today must heed his example as she constantly hears dire warnings against being dogmatic and the importance of embracing other beliefs. No matter which way the wind of opinion may blow, the church always has the same standard for her beliefs and behaviour, the eternal Word of God. The church is not free to barter this standard away so that she can be considered to be up-to-date.

The prophet of Judah had it right. He would not sit down with Jeroboam, and he would not travel the road that had brought him to Bethel. He would not do these things because he had a clear message from God that forbade him.

After the prophet of Judah departed, Jeroboam was left to contemplate what he had heard and seen. The prophet's message and confirming signs constituted more than sufficient evidence that he had been walking the path to certain disaster. In addition to these things, Jeroboam had the writings of Moses that roundly condemned idolatry. He had also had a front-row seat in viewing the ruin and disaster created by Solomon's idolatry.

All of this should have caused him to make a decisive break with his idolatry and turn to the Lord, but he refused to do so. Paul House says of the king: 'Not even a string of miracles deters Jeroboam from his path to idolatry. He still sanctions high places, non-Levitical priests, and non-Mosaic-inspired sacrifices.'[2]

As noted in the previous chapter, Scripture speaks of the 'way of Jeroboam', and ways always lead somewhere. The destination to which Jeroboam's way led was to the extinction of his house (13:34). Sad as that was, it pales in comparison with the eternal destruction into which Jeroboam was plunged when he died. That same destruction awaits all who follow in his path, as the apostle Paul clearly says idolaters will not 'inherit the kingdom of God' (1 Cor. 6:9). In building his temporal kingdom on idolatry and in refusing to turn from that idolatry, Jeroboam lost out on the eternal kingdom.

18.
The tenacity of the Word of God

Please read 1 Kings 13:11-34

The episode recorded in these verses is often considered to be one of the strangest in the Bible. This passage presents us with two prophets, one from Judah and the other from Bethel. The former is a true prophet who slips into error, and the latter is a false prophet who comes to the truth.

A casual reading of the account makes us think that we are being led up a side-trail, a very interesting one, but a side-trail none the less. It is easy to get the impression that this interesting story does not move the author forward in achieving his purpose. This will be our impression if we do not give due weight to these words: **'After this event Jeroboam did not turn from his evil way...'** (13:33). The author intended his readers to understand the story of the two prophets, not merely as an interlude, but rather as an integral part of God's dealings with Jeroboam.

We handle this account correctly, then, only if we understand that Jeroboam and his false religion are still the focus. What we are to understand from this episode is that God twice delivers his word to the rebellious king, once through the prophet from Judah and a second time through the old prophet of Bethel; once by someone from outside the northern kingdom and once by someone from within it. Jeroboam could not get away from the Word of God! The author shows us how the prophet of Bethel came to add his message to that delivered by the prophet from Judah. This is the account of a prophet who moves from compromise to truth.

A compromised and deceiving prophet (13:11-19)

'Now an old prophet dwelt in Bethel...' is the way in which the author begins this unusual story. There has been considerable conjecture about this man. Was he a prophet of the Lord who just happened to be living in Bethel when Jeroboam started his false religion? Had he, while being deeply grieved by the idolatry of Jeroboam, lacked the courage to denounce it? Or was he a Jeroboam-sympathizer?

Terence E. Fretheim, whose commentary is very helpful on this episode, observes: 'It is important to remember here that the word "prophet" is used indiscriminately for true and false prophets throughout the Old Testament ... and that prophets can move back and forth between truth and falsehood.'[1]

The old man's motive in pursuing the man of God is also uncertain. Perhaps his sons' excited recounting of what the prophet from Judah had said and done at Bethel shamed the old man. He must have seemed to his sons to be a spineless compromiser when seen alongside this stalwart prophet from Judah. If he could only persuade his fellow-prophet to come to his house, it would give him legitimacy in the eyes of his sons. Fellowship with the prophet from Judah would make it appear as if the two were on an equal footing and would lessen the gap between them in the eyes of his sons. Or he may have had a quite different motive — that is, in the words of Fretheim: ' ... to negate the word of judgement against Bethel by showing up the man of God as false'.[2]

Whatever his motive, the old prophet was desperate to bring the prophet from Judah to his home. When he succeeded in locating the man of God, he was in for a surprise. The prophet declined the invitation to come to his home because of the instructions he had received from the Lord (13:15-17).

It was at this point that the old prophet invented a lie on the spot. The Lord had sent an angel to him, he said, to countermand the instructions originally given to the prophet from Judah. It was now permissible for him to eat and drink in Bethel at the house of the old prophet.

The prophet from Judah would have done well to ponder why the Lord would suddenly begin using this old prophet as an intermediary when the Lord had started this mission by speaking directly to the prophet himself. He might have declined the old prophet's invitation by saying something like this: 'If you don't mind, I will continue on my way home until the Lord sends his angel directly to me.' He might have been suspicious about this old prophet receiving a word from God about what he was to do, when the Lord had not used this man to condemn Jeroboam's false religion. But if such thoughts passed through his mind, he quickly dismissed them and trundled off after his host (13:19). The very prophet who had been so firm and insistent with Jeroboam about the Lord's instructions fell, hook, line and sinker, for the old prophet's lie.

A truth-telling prophet (13:20-32)

God's truth for the prophet from Judah (13:20-30)

The prophet from Judah did not realize how foolish he had been until he was seated comfortably at the old prophet's table. There the latter suddenly received a startling and tragic word from the Lord. Because his guest had disobeyed his original instructions, he would not return home (13:20-22). The old prophet was not lying now. The word of the Lord had indeed come to him. The merriment of the eating and drinking must have melted very rapidly in the presence of such a shattering message. The prophet from Judah gathered his things and began his journey. He was not long on his way before a lion met him and killed him (13:23-24).

Perhaps the old prophet did not realize that his deception would lead to such a tragedy until the word of the Lord came to him at the table. The sin committed by the prophet from Judah in forsaking his original instructions may have seemed to be trifling to the old man, but it was far from that. The prophet from Judah had been used by the Lord to pronounce doom on Jeroboam for failing to obey the Word of God. Now he had failed to do the very thing for which he had condemned Jeroboam. If disobedience to God's Word merited severe judgement in the case of the king, it also merited it in the case of the prophet. It was all of one cloth.

When the old prophet heard about the death of the disobedient prophet, he went to retrieve the body. An aura of deep respect for the man of God from Judah now steals over the account. This respect is reflected first by the lion who had killed him. This lion did not eat the body, but rather stood guard over it, waiting, as it were, to be relieved from his watch by the old prophet from Bethel. When the old man arrived, the lion willingly relinquished the body (13:28-29).

The deceitful prophet from Bethel also showed deep respect for the fallen prophet from Judah. He bore his body back to Bethel, where he mourned him, perhaps out of sorrow that his own sin had led to the prophet's death, and buried him in his own tomb (13:29-30).

The old prophet also requested that his sons bury him in the same tomb (13:31) and assured them that the dead prophet's predictions would certainly come true (13:32). Those predictions did indeed come to pass and, three hundred years later, 'the men of the city' were still able to identify the tomb of the prophet from Judah (2 Kings 23:17). Such was the lasting effect of his prophecy.

Why do the closing verses of this chapter so underscore and emphasize the respect awarded this dead prophet? He did, after all, meet his death by failing to obey the Word of God. Was this man worthy of respect? Yes, because his lapse into disobedience, significant as it was, did not obliterate what had probably been a lifetime of faithful devotion to the Lord. God has no perfect servants, and sometimes he makes examples of them by severely judging their disobedience; but even when he judges he always remembers the faithful acts of his people.

God's truth for Jeroboam (13:32-34)

Through his experiences with the prophet from Judah, the old prophet of Bethel appears not only to have come to see himself as a compromiser, but also to desire to be a true prophet of the Lord. Knowing full well that Jeroboam would hear of the death of the prophet who had denounced his idolatry and that the king would be inclined to interpret the news as a sign that the prophet's message against him was false, the old man reiterated that message (13:32). The old prophet, now zealous for the truth, wanted Jeroboam to know that the Word of God stands even when God's preachers fail. The disobedience of the prophet from Judah in no way cancelled or diminished the truth of what he had said against Jeroboam.

Although Jeroboam received clear and powerful messages of warning from the two prophets in this chapter, he refused to heed them. The author simply says, **'After this event Jeroboam did not turn from his evil way... '** (13:33). How hard is the human heart!

As we have noted, the author of 1 Kings wrote to his exiled people. He shared this account of the two prophets so that these exiles would come back to their homeland with the firm and unrelenting conviction that the truthfulness of God's Word does not depend on those who declare it, but on the God who speaks it. He wanted them to come out of the exile with the knowledge that prophets come and go but the Word of God stands. The prophet Zechariah would eventually give pointed expressed to this truth:

> Your fathers, where are they?
> And the prophets, do they live for ever?
> Yet surely my words and my statutes,
> Which I commanded my servants the prophets,
> Did they not overtake your fathers?
>
> (Zech. 1:5-6).

Prophets stumble and fall, but the Word of God marches forward with unerring step. Ours is a time which sorely needs this truth. Multitudes excuse themselves from heeding the Word of God by pointing to a minister who has himself failed to live up to that Word. The apostle Paul reminds all who do this that God puts his treasure in earthen vessels (2 Cor. 4:7). The one who proclaims God's Word is always the earthen vessel — fragile and scarred — but the Word of God is the enduring treasure of inestimable value.

19.
Jeroboam, Mrs Jeroboam
and a blind prophet

Please read 1 Kings 14:1-20

With these verses the author again fastens our attention on King Jeroboam of Israel. Here the king is facing a personal crisis of the first order. His son, Abijah, was seriously ill.

Irony is to be found everywhere in this account. Jeroboam had in place an elaborate system of false religion, complete with idols and priests. But when this personal crisis arose, he sent his wife to Ahijah the prophet. When he installed his new religion, Jeroboam had appealed to the convenience of the people as a sufficient basis for embracing it, but with his own son so gravely ill, convenience was no longer a valid consideration. Although his residence at Tirzah was a good distance from the prophet's dwelling in Shiloh, Jeroboam did not think the trip was 'too much' for his wife (see 12:28).

Jeroboam's devious scheme (14:1-3)

There is no difficulty in determining why Jeroboam wanted to lay the condition of his son before Ahijah the prophet. Jeroboam had great confidence in the man. It was Ahijah who had prophesied that Jeroboam would come to the throne of Israel as a result of Solomon's idolatry (11:29-31). With the fulfilment of this prophecy an established fact, Jeroboam was sure that the prophet could accurately predict the result of his son's illness (14:3). He may even have nurtured the hope that a prophetic word from Ahijah would heal his son. But Jeroboam did not want to seek that prophetic word himself. He wanted to secure it indirectly by sending his wife. Furthermore, he wanted her to go to the prophet in disguise. The gift she bore, one which a peasant would bring (14:3), indicates that she disguised herself as a very poor woman.

Why did Jeroboam resort to this strategy? Why did he send his wife to the prophet instead of going himself? Why did he insist on disguise? Political realities must have entered into his thinking. If he or his wife were seen bypassing the priests of Bethel and going to Ahijah the prophet, the people would know that Jeroboam himself did not have confidence in the new religion that he had created.

We may also be sure that there was a significant guilt factor influencing Jeroboam's strategy. Jeroboam simply could not bring himself to face the man who had so sternly warned him to reject the idolatry that would wreck the kingdom of Solomon (11:38). Jeroboam did not even want the prophet to know that it was his wife who was seeking Ahijah's help. Therefore, she would go in disguise and the prophet would utter the prophetic word without even knowing to whom he was speaking.

Jeroboam's scheme is a very powerful warning to us about the temptation to divide God up into compartments. He wanted God's compassion for his personal crisis, but he did not want to order his life in accordance with God's commandments. How easy it is for us to follow his example! How easy it is to desire God's blessings while despising his commandments!

Jeroboam's inconsistency (14:4-6)

With a little reflection Jeroboam and his wife could very easily have seen the glaring contradiction in their scheme. They expected the prophet to see into the future without seeing through Mrs Jeroboam's disguise! That contradiction became apparent the moment she arrived at the prophet's door. Ahijah was now blind, a condition of which Jeroboam and his wife were evidently unaware, but he did not need sight to identify Jeroboam's wife. He did not even need to hear her voice. Before she arrived the Lord had told him that she was coming and why (14:5). Although Ahijah could not see, that great watcher of men, the Lord, could and did.

Ahijah's prophecy (14:6-18)

The Lord did more than merely disclose to Ahijah the identity of his disguised visitor. He also gave the prophet **'bad news'** to share with her (14:6). This bad news consisted of three parts.

The destruction of Jeroboam's house (14:6-11,14)

The first part of Ahijah's message pertained to Jeroboam's house. This same prophet had promised that the Lord would give Jeroboam an 'enduring house' if he would only walk in obedience to the Lord's commands (11:38). The completeness of Jeroboam's failure to do so was set out by Ahijah in devastating terms. Jeroboam had not only failed to follow the example of David (14:8), but had done more evil than all who had preceded him. Specifically, he had made **'other gods and moulded images'** and had cast God behind his back (14:9).

Such high-handed and hard-hearted disobedience meant that Jeroboam had forfeited the enduring house promised by the Lord. His whole house was now to be wiped out and this would come about in a most shameful and ignominious way: they would be eaten by dogs and birds (14:10-11). To die in such a way, without mourners and burial, was considered a sign of immense disgrace and disrespect.

This destruction was to be carried out by a king whom the Lord would raise up, that is, Baasha (15:27-30), and it was to happen soon. The words, **'... this is the day. What? Even now!'** (14:14) may have referred to the son, Abijah, who was ill and was to die that very day — a death that Jeroboam and his wife were to regard as the first instalment of all the judgements Ahijah was announcing. Others take the phrase to mean that God had already 'set into operation those forces that would ultimately destroy the nation'.[1]

The death of Jeroboam's son (14:12-13,17-18)

After announcing the extermination of Jeroboam's entire house, the prophet Ahijah proceeded to deal specifically with the issue that had brought Jeroboam's wife to visit him. Abijah would die upon her return to Tirzah. Unlike Jeroboam's other descendants, Abijah would be buried because there was in him **'something good toward the LORD God of Israel'** (14:13). The good found in Abijah is not identified. John Gill suggests that he manifested, among other good traits, 'a dislike of idolatry, and a desire to have true religion restored'.[2]

The prophecy of Ahijah was minutely fulfilled. Abijah died at the precise moment his mother returned from Ahijah (14:17) and was mourned by the whole nation (14:18).

The captivity of Jeroboam's nation (14:15-16)

Ahijah closed his prophecy with a word about the entire nation. Because of the idolatry Jeroboam had introduced, Israel was to be uprooted and carried into captivity. This shows us that while Jeroboam was the instigator of the idolatry, the people were not without fault. They willingly followed in the way of

Jeroboam. 2 Kings 17 documents the fulfilment of this portion of Ahijah's prophecy.

Jeroboam's death (14:19-20)

The author wraps up his account of Jeroboam by introducing what is to become more or less his standard formula for summarizing the reigns of the various kings of Israel and Judah. This formula consists of: aspects of the reign not included in the author's account; other sources of information; length of reign; death and burial; and succession.[3]

It is interesting that it is only in this summary that the author refers to the wars of Jeroboam. We might have expected these wars to have been reported at some length, but they are only mentioned in passing. The author's purpose in writing, as we noted at the outset, was not to provide a blow-by-blow history, but rather to provide a spiritual understanding of it. He did not report the wars of Jeroboam because they paled in comparison with the idolatry that the king had introduced into Israel. That was the feature of his reign that continued to influence Israel until her captivity.

While Jeroboam has long since passed off the stage of history, he still speaks to us about the importance of shunning idols and living on the basis of God's Word.

Secondly, he has much to say to us about the very crucial matter of influence. Jeroboam's decision to set up his false religion continued to exert a powerful influence on the kingdom of Israel until she ceased to be a kingdom, and we may be sure that our failures to follow the Lord wholly can send out ripples in many lives and often over a period of many years.

Thirdly, Jeroboam serves as a warning to us of the certainty of God's judgement on those who disdain his ways and disregard his truth.

No life makes for sadder reading than that of Jeroboam. We should be thankful that we can lay alongside it the life of the Lord Jesus Christ. In Christ we find a heart totally devoted to God and a life unstained by disobedience. Because of his fidelity to God and to the work God gave him to do, his people find forgiveness of sins and title to eternal glory.

20.
Two idolatrous reigns in Judah

Please read 1 Kings 14:21 - 15:8

Having detailed the disastrous course established by Jeroboam in the kingdom of Israel, the author turns his attention to describe briefly the reigns of two idolatrous kings in Judah: Rehoboam and Abijam.

We may find it somewhat surprising that Rehoboam plunged into idolatry. The results of Solomon's idolatry were all too plain. The nation was rent in two just as God had said it would be. One would think, therefore, that Rehoboam would have been quick to learn from Solomon's folly and would have solemnly resolved to have nothing whatsoever to do with idols.

Rehoboam appears to have indeed made this his resolve in the early part of his reign. The author of 2 Chronicles tells us that he 'forsook the law of the LORD' after he had 'established the kingdom' and had 'strengthened himself' (2 Chr. 12:1).

When Rehoboam did plunge into idolatry, he did so on an unprecedented scale. The author of 1 Kings says the sins of the people of Judah were at this time **'more than all that their fathers had done'** (14:22). The sad reality that his son Abijam followed his example provides eloquent testimony to the importance of fathers setting the proper example for their children.

The idolatrous reign of Rehoboam (14:21-31)

The nature of the idolatry (14:23-24)

Verses 23-24 give us the author's snapshot of Rehoboam's idolatry. The **'high places'** were the elevated places in which the worship of idols was carried out. **'Every green tree'** suggests that these high places were covered with groves. The trees themselves may very well have been considered to be symbols of fertility and were thus fitting emblems of a religion that featured sexual rites and sought to ensure fertility. The **'sacred pillars'** and **'wooden images'** were the material representations of gods. Some think the former represented male deities while the latter represented female deities. The **'perverted persons in the land'** is a reference to the prostitutes who were present at these places of worship. With such prostitutes on hand, the worshippers could re-enact the supposed sexual coupling of the gods themselves and, in so doing, secure fertility.

None of this was new. These were the religious practices of the Canaanite nations who possessed the land before the Lord gave it to Israel, practices that caused the Lord to drive those nations out of the land (14:24).

Before driving these nations out, the Lord had made it abundantly plain to his people that they must not repeat the sinful practices of the Canaanites. Their wickedness caused them to be driven out, and that same wickedness in his people would be visited with the same judgement.

What possessed Rehoboam, in the light of what the Lord had done with the Canaanite nations and of what idolatry had already cost his kingdom, to lead his people into idolatry? The author does not explicitly state a reason. It is interesting, however, that he twice mentions Rehoboam's mother, Naamah, an

Ammonitess (14: 21,31). We know Solomon's many wives 'turned his heart after other gods' (11:4). We should not be surprised if one of these women, Rehoboam's mother, had the same effect upon her son.

The results of the idolatry (14:25-26)

We read the account of Rehoboam's flagrant idolatry with a sense of expectancy, waiting, as it were, for the other shoe to drop, and drop it does in verse 25: **'It happened in the fifth year of King Rehoboam that Shishak king of Egypt came up against Jerusalem.'**

By saying 'it happened', the author does not mean to suggest that this event was just an unfortunate circumstance that came about by chance. No, he was much too convinced of God's sovereignty in history to allow for that. It 'happened' because the Lord designed it to happen. The Lord brought Shishak of Egypt against Jerusalem as a judgement upon Rehoboam (2 Chr. 12:2,5)

Once in Jerusalem, Shishak and his army removed all the valuables from the house of the Lord and from the king's house, including the shields of gold that Solomon had made (14:26; 2 Chr. 9:15-16). These shields were of particular interest to our author. He may have regarded them as symbols both of the glory of the kingdom and God's protective care of it, and Shishak's taking of them as a particularly powerful representation of lost glory and lost protection.

Rehoboam's response (14:27-28)

How did Rehoboam respond to this invasion? After Shishak had departed, treasures in hand, the king made more shields, not of gold, but rather of bronze (14:27), a telling symbol of the terrible deterioration that his idolatry had created. And, as if these cheap substitutes were in even more danger of being spirited away than those of gold, Rehoboam instituted some very elaborate procedures for guarding them (14:27-28; 2 Chr. 12:10-11).

In the space of a few short years, Judah had gone from gold to bronze. This was not to be explained in terms of the natural life-cycle of the kingdom. It was rather because the leaders and the people had 'transgressed against the LORD' (2 Chr. 12:2,5). This account serves to remind us that disobedience to God always leads to deterioration. It takes us from gold to bronze.

The book of 2 Chronicles makes it clear that the invasion of Shishak caused Rehoboam and the leaders of Judah to come temporarily to their senses. The author of 2 Chronicles writes, 'So the leaders of Israel and the king humbled themselves; and they said, "The LORD is righteous"' (2 Chr. 12:6).

Because they humbled themselves the Lord granted them 'some deliverance' (2 Chr. 12:7), in that he did not allow Shishak to devastate the land completely. They did, however, become Shishak's vassals, so the Lord could make them 'distinguish' his service from the service of the nations' (2 Chr. 12:8); that is, so they could learn that it was far better to serve God.

It must be noted that Rehoboam and his leaders only temporarily came to their senses and acknowledged the Lord. There was no deep and abiding repentance that drove them to purge the land of idolatry. If Rehoboam's turning to the Lord had been genuine and lasting, the author of 2 Chronicles would not have found it necessary to summarize his reign by saying, 'He did evil' (2 Chr. 12:14).

The idolatrous reign of Abijam (15:1-8)

On Rehoboam's death his son Abijam came to the throne. In his brief account of Abijam's reign, the author calls our attention to three things: the name of his mother (15:2), his idolatry (15:3-5) and his continual war with Jeroboam and the northern kingdom (15:6).

Abijam's mother, Maachah (15:2)

The double mention of his mother Maachah in this chapter (15:2,10) indicates that she was a very strong woman who exerted considerable influence, an influence that was obviously evil and idolatrous (15:13).

Abijam's idolatry (15:3-5)

It is the matter of Abijam's idolatry that receives most of the author's emphasis. To put it bluntly, Abijam not only followed his father to the throne, but also followed his idolatry. How careful parents must be about the example they set and the spiritual legacy they leave! The fact that Abijam was on the throne was a testimony to the good spiritual legacy of his great-grandfather David (15:3-5). The fact that he used that throne to promote idolatry was a testimony to the wicked legacy of his father. The only real connection between Abijam and David was mere physical descent. He was a stranger to David's heart of loyal devotion to the Lord.

Abijam's commitment to idols may very well have been reflected by the change in his name. At the beginning of his reign, he had the name 'Abijah' (2 Chr. 13:1-2), which is not to be confused with Jeroboam's son with the same name (14:1).

A name such as 'Abijah' ('My father is the LORD') must have felt strangely unfitting to him as he worshipped his false gods, so he set it aside in favour of 'Abijam' ('father of the sea').

Abijam's conflict with Jeroboam (15:6)

The third point of emphasis in this account is Abijam's ongoing conflict with Jeroboam. While this account only makes passing reference to it, the author of 2 Chronicles gives details of a resounding victory enjoyed by Abijam and his forces.

Before the battle started, Abijam delivered a very fine-sounding speech in which he rebuked Israel for idolatry while claiming that his kingdom, Judah, was staying true to the Lord (2 Chr. 13:4-12). It was true, of course, that Judah was still outwardly maintaining the temple worship, as Abijam claimed (2 Chr. 13:10-11). What he conveniently forgot to mention was that the worship of idols was being carried on right alongside the worship of God. And there can never be any real worship of God if the worship of any other god is placed alongside it.

The Lord gave Abijam and Judah the victory over Jeroboam and Israel on that day, but the reason was not, as Abijam insisted, that he and his people were being faithful to the Lord. It was rather because they relied on God on that specific occasion (2 Chr. 13:18), and the Lord wanted to give them a tangible indication of the blessings that would be theirs if they would break with their idols and rely on him on all occasions.

This business of breaking with idols is the very message we ourselves need to hear. Our idols are no less idols because they are more sophisticated and intangible than those of Rehoboam and Abijam, and every idol, sophisticated or not, is extremely displeasing to the Lord and invites his judgement.

The sad spectacle of Rehoboam and Abijam plummeting into idolatry should fill our hearts with gratitude for the Lord Jesus Christ. One of the temptations consisted of Satan's showing him the kingdoms of the world and saying, 'All these things I will give you if you will fall down and worship me.' The Lord responded by saying, 'Away with you, Satan! For it is written, "You shall worship the LORD your God, and him only you shall serve"' (Matt. 4:8-10). Because of that unwavering loyalty to the Father, our Saviour was able to provide redemption for all who believe.

21.
A powerful reign with a pitiful end

Please read 1 Kings 15:9-24

The nation of Judah was in desperate need of a good king when Asa came along. His great-grandfather Solomon, his grandfather Rehoboam and his father Abijam had all contributed to the widespread idolatry of the nation. Solomon had planted the seeds, and Rehoboam and Abijam had watered them. When Asa came along the crop of idolatry was exceedingly bountiful.

It is often the case that children follow in the footsteps of their parents, but Asa was an exception to the rule. Many in Judah probably thought Asa's reign would only bring them more of the same, but if so they were wrong. Let's learn from this that the grace of God can change seemingly hopeless situations.

Asa's powerful reign

Asa wasted very little time in addressing the idolatrous worship his predecessors had put in place. He banished the cult prostitutes from the land and removed all the idols (15:12). He even went so far as to remove his grandmother Maachah as queen mother. The obscene image she had made suggests that she may very well have been the primary promoter of idolatry in the land. Asa's commitment to the Lord was such that he could not tolerate his grandmother or her idol (15:13).

The only flaw to be found in Asa's attack on the idolatry of the land is that he left the **'high places'** (15:14). This seems to be in conflict with what we are told in 2 Chronicles 14:5, namely, that Asa 'removed the high places and the incense altars from all the cities of Judah'. If the author of 2 Chronicles had made the statement that Asa removed *all* the high places, there would be a contradiction, but he did not. What we are to understand, then, is that while Asa removed some, perhaps even most, of the high places, his work was not so thorough as to eliminate all of them. Thus he could simultaneously be commended for removing the high places (2 Chr. 14:5) and condemned for not removing all of them (1 Kings 15:14; 2 Chr. 15:17). John Gill resolves the conflict by suggesting that Asa removed the high places that had been used for idolatrous worship but not those that had been used for the worship of the Lord.[1]

Although Asa's reforming work was not as complete as it should have been in regard to the high places, the author of 1 Kings is still able to say that his heart was **'loyal to the Lord all his days'** (15:14).

In addition to largely purging the land of the trappings of idol worship, Asa gave himself to restoring the worship of the Lord. He replenished the temple with silver and gold utensils (15:15; 2 Chr. 15:18) and convened a great assembly for the purpose of entering into a covenant to seek the Lord (2 Chr. 15:10-15).

Asa's pitiful end

It all amounted to a much-needed and very refreshing change for the kingdom of Judah, and we could wish that the story of Asa's reign ended with this change, but it does not. Towards the end of his reign (after thirty-five years of his forty-one year reign), Asa astonishingly turned away from the very thing that had so characterized and distinguished the first part of his reign, that is, dependence on the Lord.

The threat of Baasha (15:16-17)

The event that precipitated this turning was the decision of Baasha, King of Israel, to fortify Ramah. Asa's reforms in Judah had proved to be like a magnet to those in Israel who were sick of their diet of idolatry. The author of 2 Chronicles says people came to Asa 'in great numbers from Israel when they saw that the LORD his God was with him' (2 Chr. 15:9). This was more than Baasha could bear. Ramah, approximately two hours' march from Jerusalem, commanded the road to the city and was the perfect place for Baasha to fortify.

On a previous occasion, Asa had faced a foe much stronger than himself, the Ethiopians, and had sought the face of the Lord with this urgent prayer: 'LORD, it is nothing for you to help, whether with many or with those who have no power; help us, O LORD our God, for we rest on you, and in your name we go against this multitude. O LORD, you are our God; do not let man prevail against you!' (2 Chr. 14:11). The Lord had answered that prayer by giving Asa and his army a stunning and glorious victory over the Ethiopians (2 Chr. 14:12-15).

The strategy of Asa (15:18-22)

But now, with Baasha posing a threat and with the very same God on the throne, Asa did not resort to the Lord. Instead he formed a treaty with Ben-Hadad of Syria and persuaded him with silver and gold to divert Baasha's attention away from Ramah (15:18-19). This Ben-Hadad did by attacking several cities in Israel (15:20-21). While Baasha was occupied with these attacks, Asa tore down his fortifications at Ramah and used the materials for a couple of building projects of his own (15:22).

The displeasure of the Lord

Asa's strategy may appear to us to have been innocent enough, but it was far from it. And a prophet of the Lord, Hanani, let Asa know in no uncertain terms that his course had displeased the Lord: 'Because you have relied on the king of Syria, and have not relied on the Lord your God, therefore the army of the king of Syria has escaped from your hand. Were the Ethiopians and the Lubim not a huge army with very many chariots and horsemen? Yet, because you relied on the Lord, he delivered them into your hand. For the eyes of the Lord run to and fro throughout the whole earth, to show himself strong on behalf of those whose heart is loyal to him. In this you have done foolishly; therefore from now on you shall have wars' (2 Chr. 16:7-9).

Asa's response to the Word of the Lord

Hanani's stern message was met with yet another evidence that Asa had dramatically drifted from the Lord. Instead of giving the prophet a submissive hearing and falling on his face in genuine repentance, Asa became so angry that he had Hanani imprisoned. And he also began to treat his own people in an oppressive manner (2 Chr. 16:10).

On a previous occasion, Asa had heeded a message from Azariah, another prophet of the Lord, and had been blessed of the Lord as a result (2 Chr. 15:1-9). But by the time Hanani came along, Asa's attitude towards the Word of God had drastically changed.

Asa's refusal to seek the Lord did not come to an end with the Baasha affair. When he was afflicted with a serious illness, he sought the help of physicians rather than the help of the

Lord (2 Chr. 16:12). We should not take this as a blanket indictment on seeking medical help. The fact that Luke in the New Testament was a physician is enough to tell us that the Lord approves of physicians and employs them for the treatment and healing of disease. But Asa's case was special. His sickness had come upon him as a result of the deterioration of his faith and as a means of testing him to see if he would again rely upon the Lord. He failed the test.

Points of special application

Faithfulness to the end

The life of Asa abounds with spiritual lessons for each and every child of God, but some shine more clearly than others. One of these has to do with the importance of being faithful to the end. We never walk with the Lord so long that we are beyond the possibility of grievous sin. We can put it in another way: as long as we are in this life we shall have enemies devoted to destroying our spiritual progress and usefulness. We must ever be on our guard against the world, the flesh and the devil.

This lesson is poignantly presented by the lives of other men. Simon Peter enjoyed the closest possible association with Jesus during the latter's public ministry, and at the very end of that time, Simon Peter denied his Lord three times (Matt. 26:69-75). Still later, he publicly compromised on the key doctrine of justification by faith alone by refusing to eat with Gentile believers at Antioch (Gal. 2:11-21).

David walked with the Lord for so many years that he would seem to have been beyond all danger, but he let his guard down and descended into sexual immorality, murder and deception (2 Sam. 11:1-27).

On guard against the world

Another point of application comes from remembering the nature of what Asa did in his latter years. After exercising dependence on the Lord in things great and small throughout his early years, he failed to seek the Lord regarding Baasha and relied on Syria instead. Asa's life reminds us, then, to be especially alert to the danger of being infatuated with worldly wisdom.

This is where many churches, pastors and individual Christians find themselves today. There was a time when they heartily embraced every doctrine of the historic Christian faith, but the relentless pounding of public opinion against these doctrines has left them tongue-tied and hesitant to boldly assert those very doctrines. The preaching of the cross has always been foolish to the natural man, but many Christians today seem to be unwilling to appear as fools for believing and preaching it.

Loving the Word of God

A final point of application may be stated in this way: our attitude to the Word of God is a key element in maintaining our faithfulness to the Lord. As we have noted, there was a time when Asa loved the Word of God and submitted to its message, but somewhere along the line his attitude shifted so far that he imprisoned Hanani for faithfully declaring it. Our great safeguard is ever the Word of God. It has a way of discovering our sins and correcting us. When there is a heart-shift away from that Word, we close the door to correction and open it to disaster. We must always, therefore, carefully examine ourselves to see if we are maintaining a tender disposition towards God's Word.

22.
Vital lessons from vile kings

Please read 1 Kings 15:25 - 16:34

These are days in which we are extremely reluctant to call anyone evil. Professor Alan Bloom once asked a class of undergraduates to name someone they thought was evil. None of the students could identify an evil person.[1]

The author of 1 Kings had no such hesitancy. In these verses he turns our attention away from the kingdom of Judah and focuses again on the kingdom of Israel. In rapid-fire succession he briefly describes the reigns of five of Israel's kings before going into detail about the sixth. It makes for very depressing reading. These were all extremely bad kings. They were not bad in the sense of being poor administrators, or inept politicians. They were spiritually bad. Without regard to God or his laws, they plunged themselves and their nation deeper and deeper into idolatry and deeper and deeper into trouble. The names of these six kings, with the possible exception of the last, are not well known to people in general, but they all have stars affixed to them in the annals of hell. These men are heroes there because they excelled in evil.

The vile kings

Nadab (15:25-32)

Nadab was the first of these kings. He followed his father Jeroboam not only to the throne but also into idolatry (15:26). While he was involved in the siege of Gibbethon, one of his officers, Baasha, brought his two-year reign to an end by assassinating him (15:27). Baasha also killed all of Nadab's family and, in so doing, brought the prophecy of Ahijah to fulfilment (15:29; cf. 14:10).

Baasha (15:33 - 16:7)

Baasha's assassination of Nadab was not prompted by any hatred of his sin or by a zeal to see Israel turn to God. On the contrary, Baasha himself **'walked in the way of Jeroboam'** (15:34). His reign, the third longest in the history of Israel after its split from Judah, lasted for twenty-four years, but all through those years Baasha gave himself to idolatry. Because he followed Jeroboam's sin he was, according to Jehu the prophet, to share Jeroboam's fate (16:1-4).

Elah (16:8-14)

Baasha's son, Elah, succeeded his father but reigned for less than two years. While Israel's army was engaged at Gibbethon (16:15), Elah was **'drinking himself drunk'** in Tirzah (16:9). He was assassinated by Zimri, the **'commander of half his chariots'** (16:9), who also killed all the members of his family and thus fulfilled to the letter the prophecy of Jehu (16:11-13).

Zimri (16:15-20)

Zimri holds the distinction of having the shortest reign in the history of Israel — seven days (16:15). His assassination of Elah sparked civil unrest in Israel. Omri, the commander of the army, was selected as king by **'all Israel'**, evidently a reference to the army and the leaders of Israel who were present at Gibbethon. Omri responded to his selection by leading the army away from there to Tirzah, where Zimri was. When Zimri saw that he had no chance of succeeding against Omri, he **'burned the king's house down upon himself'** (16:18).

Although Zimri only reigned for seven days, the author accuses him of **'walking in the way of Jeroboam'** (16:19). This suggests that he was an inveterate and well-known idolater before he became king and would most certainly have led Israel to continue her idolatrous ways.

Omri (16:21-28)

The army's selection of Omri and Zimri's subsequent suicide did not mean that the former's path to the throne was cleared. For a period of four years, Israel was torn into factions — one following Omri and the other Tibni. The struggle came to an end when Tibni died (16:21-22). No cause is assigned for his death, but it would not be surprising if Omri were responsible for it.

Omri's reign was distinguished by two things. First, he built the city of Samaria on a hill which he purchased from a man named 'Shemer', and made it the capital of Israel. Secondly, he gave himself to evil in an unprecedented way. It seems that with each of these kings Israel was going from bad to worse. With Omri they had a king who **'did worse than all who were before him'** (16:25). Omri **'walked in all the ways of Jeroboam the son of Nebat, and in his sin...'** (16:26).

Ahab (16:29-34)

After a reign of six years Omri died and was succeeded by his
son Ahab. His is one of the most stained names in all of Scripture. It is not difficult to see why. Under him the nation so
continued its downward spiral that he took the distinction pre-
viously awarded to his father as the most evil of Israel's kings
(16:30,33).

The author documents this claim by citing five features of
Ahab's reign.

First, like his predecessors, he continued to **'walk in
the sins of Jeroboam'** (16:31).

Secondly, he married Jezebel, the daughter of the King
of the Sidonians (16:31).

Thirdly, he passionately promoted the worship of
Baal, both building a temple for him and consecrating
an altar to him (16:32).

Fourthly, Ahab made a **'wooden image'** (16:32), a
lewd representation of a female deity carved from a
wooden pole.

Finally, during Ahab's reign, Hiel of Bethel rebuilt
the walls of the city of Jericho. Those walls had col-
lapsed when God gave the city to Israel during the time
of Joshua, and God had made it abundantly clear that
they were never to be rebuilt (Josh. 6:26). But contempt
for the Word of God was so pronounced during the reign
of Ahab that Hiel did not hesitate to undertake this
project. Hiel paid a fearful price for his defiance of God's
Word, losing his eldest son with the laying of the foundation and his youngest with the setting of the gates
(16:34). This fulfilment of God's word to Joshua showed
that God's Word cannot be destroyed but only confirmed.

The vital lessons

Scripture does not record the brief summaries of the reigns of these kings merely to satisfy those who have an interest in ancient history. They are included to further the Bible's purpose of benefiting us spiritually (1 Cor. 10:11; 2 Tim. 3:16-17). Two lessons of enormous spiritual value emerge from these summaries.

The reliability of God's Word

One of these is the total reliability of the Word of God. Baasha reigns and the prophecy of Ahijah is fulfilled (15:29). Zimri comes to the throne and the prophecy of Jehu is fulfilled (16:12). Hiel rebuilds the walls of Jericho and the word of the Lord to Joshua is fulfilled (16:34). These instances constitute only a meagre sampling on this matter. The Bible is full of examples of this very thing. Because God so jealously guarded the integrity of his Word through the centuries covered by the Bible, we may rest assured that he will continue to do so. The promises of Scripture regarding the coming of Christ, eternal destruction for unbelievers and eternal glory for the saints will all be fulfilled. And when the saints of God are finally home and look back upon human history they will join Joshua in testifying to the faithfulness of God to his Word: '... not one thing has failed of all the good things which the LORD your God spoke concerning you. All have come to pass for you; not one word of them has failed' (Josh. 23:14).

The folly of rebelling against God's Word

This lesson, the reliability of God's Word, inevitably yields yet another, that is, the utter folly of ignoring that Word and rebelling against it.

The Lord spoke very pointedly to Israel during the time of Moses about the terrible sin of idolatry. He warned Jeroboam, the initiator of idolatry in Israel, on more than one occasion about the terrible nature of what he was doing and where it would lead (11:33,38; 13:1-5; 14:1-16). He pronounced doom upon Baasha for following the path of Jeroboam (16:1-4). And when Israel was at her lowest ebb under the vile Ahab, the Lord sent the great prophet Elijah to show the king the folly of his course. But without exception these men refused to heed the warnings of the Lord and continued in their idolatrous ways. In so doing they brought immeasurable pain upon themselves and their nation.

It is easy enough to see the chaos and turmoil of Israel during these years, but these men and those who followed them paid an even heavier price than what meets the eye in these accounts. In turning to idols, they turned away from the hope of Israel, the coming Messiah, and in that turning brought upon themselves the far greater agony of eternal destruction.

The Lord himself decreed the division of the kingdom into Israel and Judah, but this did not mean that the kings and the people of Israel were free to completely turn their backs upon the house of David that ruled in Judah. The Lord had promised that the Messiah would spring from David's line and that the division of the kingdom was for the purpose of temporarily afflicting the house of David (11:39). The kings of Israel appear to have taken the division as a licence to make a total break with the house of David, including abandoning the Messianic hope. What a fearful price they paid for giving up this hope!

The Messiah towards whom the Old Testament points did come. Eternal salvation still rests upon receiving him in faith. Those who refuse this message join the sad company of these kings who refused to look forward in faith to the coming Christ. It is the company of the damned.

23.
Elijah before Ahab and at Cherith

Please read 1 Kings 17:1-7

With this chapter the author shifts his focus from kings and their reigns to the prophets of God, and especially the great Elijah. He sets the stage for Elijah's appearance with these ominous words about Ahab: '... and he went and served Baal and worshipped him' (16:31).

We should not conclude from these words that Ahab worshipped Baal exclusively. The names of his children (Ahaziah, Jehoram and Athaliah) show that he still retained at least a nominal allegiance to God because each included an element of the Hebrew name for God. Ahab was a syncretist. He believed that both Baal and God could be worshipped, each in his own sphere, without doing violence to either; that it was not necessary to make a choice between the two.

Baal was the nature god of the Canaanite nations and Phoenicia. Although he was worshipped with many local titles (e.g. Baal-Gad, Baal-Hermon, Baal-Zephon), one feature was constant and unchanging — namely, that he was responsible for rainfall, an extremely crucial matter for agricultural nations such as Israel and her neighbours.

The fact that Israel and the surrounding nations did experience a seasonal lack of rain was explained by Baal-worshippers in this way: each year Baal submitted to Mot, the god of death, and in so doing brought drought and barrenness. Yet another god, Anat, would eventually free Baal by defeating Mot, and Baal would then send rain and restore fertility to the land.[1]

Worship of Baal had existed in Israel long before Ahab ever came to the throne (Judg. 2:11,13; 3:7; 10:6,10; 1 Sam. 12:10), but Ahab gave it, in the words of the *MacArthur Study Bible*, 'official sanction' by building a temple for Baal in Samaria, the capital of Israel.[2]

Why did Ahab so vigorously promote the worship of Baal? The answer lies in one of the most sinister and vile characters in all of Scripture: his wife Jezebel (16:31). Jezebel was the daughter of Ethbaal, King of the Sidonians, which is synonymous with the Phoenicians. Unlike her husband, Jezebel was no syncretist. She was totally and radically devoted to the worship of Baal and to the complete eradication of the worship of God.

Elijah appears before Ahab (17:1)

His message

Against this backdrop, the prophet Elijah suddenly appears in Ahab's court. We are not told anything about him except that he was **'of the inhabitants of Gilead'** (17:1). It is possible that he was dwelling in this neighbouring country with many other Israelites because of the pressure placed on the faithful by Ahab. The author does not explain Elijah's connection with Gilead. It is as if the situation in Israel was so desperate and urgent that the author could not be detained by giving biographical information about the prophet.

Neither are we told exactly how Elijah came to confront Ahab. Did he encounter him as the king was travelling around his kingdom? Did he simply walk unannounced into his court?

The author does not say. His emphasis is on the message that Elijah delivered. It was indeed an unadorned, straightforward message: **'As the LORD God of Israel lives, before whom I stand, there shall not be dew nor rain these years, except at my word'** (17:1).

Perhaps Ahab turned to his servants as the prophet strode away and asked for his name. He may even have experienced a sickening feeling as he heard the reply: 'O king, that was the prophet Elijah.' That name, 'My God is Jehovah,' along with Elijah's message, would have left no doubt in the minds of Ahab and those around him about what had taken place. War had just been declared on Ahab's storm-god Baal and all his devotees. Elijah had declared that it was the God of Israel who determined rain and gave fertility to the land. Rainfall was part of God's sovereign control and part of his covenant with Israel (Lev. 26:3-5; Deut. 11:13-17; 28:12) and he was not about to share his throne, or his prerogatives, with another. More than that, Elijah's God was the one who had delivered Israel from Egypt and had commanded that his people were to have no other gods and make no images (Exod. 20:1-6; Deut. 5:6-10), but were to love and serve him, and him alone (Deut. 6:5,13-15).

His faith

Elijah's message reverberated with conviction. He allowed himself no room at all for wiggling out of a tight situation, but in no uncertain terms categorically declared a drought for Israel. How did Elijah come to such a strong and unequivocal position? Was this a 'name and claim it' proposition which the prophet staked out because he had convinced himself that it would be true? Is faith just a matter of our choosing to believe something and believing it so strongly that we somehow activate latent powers and cause the thing believed to come to pass? These popular notions of faith are far removed from Elijah's faith.

In announcing the drought he was acting on the basis of the revealed Word of God. It was God who, through Moses, had given Israel notice that one of the judgements for idolatry would be drought: 'Take heed to yourselves, lest your heart be deceived, and you turn aside and serve other gods and worship them, lest the LORD's anger be aroused against you, and he shut up the heavens so that there be no rain...' (Deut. 11:16-17).

Elijah had not only read that word but also unwaveringly believed it and, in going to Ahab, acted upon it. The author of the book of James writes of Elijah, 'He prayed earnestly that it would not rain; and it did not rain on the land for three years and six months' (James 5:17). Here is an example of 'the prayer of faith' (James 5:15). It is not praying for anything we want and trying to convince ourselves that we shall have it because we really do believe it. No, it is praying on the basis of God's revealed truth.

Faith is not believing anything we choose to believe. It is believing what God has said. On the basis of what he found in the writings of Moses, Elijah began to pray that God would do in Israel what he had promised.

Some find a contradiction between the phrase 'in the third year' (18:1) and the 'three years and six months' mentioned by James (James 5:17; see also Luke 4:25). There is, however, no conflict here. If we assume that the drought had already begun before Elijah appeared before Ahab, we can accommodate the three and a half years to which James refers. In all likelihood, Elijah went to Ahab after taking note of the developing drought and after being convinced that God had indeed heard his prayers and was already in the process of fulfilling the word he had spoken through Moses. Elijah could then go to Ahab without the slightest degree of hesitancy or uncertainty.

Elijah goes to Cherith (17:2-7)

In addition to having the revealed Word of God in the writings of Moses, Elijah was himself a recipient of divine revelation. After he appeared to Ahab, the Lord instructed him to hide himself by the Brook Cherith where he would be able to drink from the brook and be fed by the ravens (17:3-4).

Elijah's experience at Cherith has sometimes been used as evidence that the people of God today can expect God to perform miracles on their behalf just as he did on behalf of the prophet. It is true, of course, that God does care for the needs of his people (Phil. 4:19), and when it suits him he can certainly perform miracles. But there is more to Cherith than this. God did not take Elijah there merely to show that he can miraculously provide for his people. The significance of Cherith lay in God's graciously affirming some vital lessons for the prophet:

1. The fact that God used the ravens to bring food to Elijah, food that they would naturally have eaten themselves, confirmed for him that God, not Baal, controls nature. God graciously provides confirmation for our faith even when our faith is strong and, in so doing, keeps faith strong and growing.

2. The fact that Elijah was at this particular time the vehicle, and we might say, the embodiment of the Word of God, and that God was miraculously caring for him, was proof that God will always sustain his Word. By caring for the vehicle of his Word, Elijah, God was showing the prophet that he need not tremble at the final outcome of the struggle with Baal. God's Word would finally prevail.

3. The fact that God was providing food and water for Elijah, while withholding it from the nation in general,

showed that his covenant blessings were for the obedient (Elijah) and not for the disobedient (Israel in general).

4. The fact that God sustained Elijah at Cherith must have encouraged the exiles in Babylon to believe that God would sustain them as well.

Practical lessons

We do well if we come away from Elijah's sudden appearance before Ahab and his hiding at Cherith with the following lessons indelibly etched on our minds:

1. God abominates any attempt at syncretism. He and he alone is to be the object of our worship and the focus of our service. It is, therefore, vitally important for God's people to be ever vigilant against attempts to incorporate into the Christian faith the findings of the latest opinion poll. No one can serve two masters (Matt. 6:24). Christians should also diligently avoid deep and intimate relationships with people who, like Jezebel, are totalitarian in their devotion to false gods and desire the obliteration of 'the faith which was once for all delivered to the saints' (Jude 3).

2. While Christians are not called to be prophets in the same sense that Elijah was, we are all called to affirm steadfastly in times of evil that our God is Jehovah.

3. While evil times often make it seem that God's cause is lost, we can rest assured that God will honour his Word and sustain his cause.

24.
Elijah at the widow's house

Please read 1 Kings 17:8-24

God could very easily have sustained Elijah at Cherith even after the brook dried up. The ravens that carried food could just as easily have carried containers of water. The God who quenched the thirst of a multitude by causing water to burst forth from a rock (Exod. 17:1-6; Num. 20:7-11) would have had no trouble providing water for a solitary prophet. Elijah left Cherith, not because of necessity, but rather because God wanted him to go to Zarephath.

At Zarephath the prophet encountered a destitute widow and her son and performed two miracles on their behalf. These are Elijah's first recorded miracles.

The multiplication of the widow's food (17:8-16)

While Elijah was still at Cherith the Lord told him to go to Zarephath where he would find a widow who had been **'com-manded'** to provide for him (17:9). There is no reason to believe that this woman was at the time a believer in the God of Israel. When Elijah encountered her, she referred to his God but gave no indication that she shared his faith (17:12). It would not be long before she did.

Here then is the sovereignty of God at work. The Lord had chosen this woman before she was ever aware of it and had given her a disposition to respond kindly to Elijah. This is always God's way. All those who are saved were chosen by him long before they ever became aware of it, and all who are saved manifest God's work in their hearts by a disposition that kindly receives the Word of God.

The widow's response indicated just how strongly God had worked in her heart. She and her son were down to a mere handful of flour and a drop of oil and, when Elijah found her, she was gathering sticks to build a fire so she could make a little cake. She and her son would share that meagre meal and then wait to die because she had absolutely no hope of securing any resources for the future (17:12).

Such a sad and depressing account would make any of us apologize for asking, as Elijah had done, for a cup of water and a piece of bread (17:11). We would have whispered our condolences and best wishes and gone on our way. But not Elijah. He asked the woman to make her cake and give it to him! Why would the prophet make such an unfeeling and harsh demand? It was because he had a promise from God to place alongside the demand. If this woman would give her all to the prophet, she would find meal in her barrel and oil in her jar until the drought finally released its grip (17:14).

On one hand the woman had her meagre resources. On the other hand she had the promise of God. Would she cling to her resources, meagre as they were, or would she cling to the Word of God? The author gives us the answer: **'So she went away and did according to the word of Elijah...'** (17:15).

The author also shares the blessed sequel: **'... and she and he and her household ate for many days. The bin of flour was not used up, nor did the jar of oil run dry, according to the word of the Lord which he spoke by Elijah'** (17:16).

It must have seemed to the widow that she was giving up so very much to honour the Word of God, but she was really only giving up a tiny bit of meal and oil. It was all she had, but it was temporary and perishing, and by giving it up in obedience to God she received that which was lasting. In like manner, the gospel of Jesus Christ demands that we give ourselves up to it totally so that we may receive that life which is eternal.

The resurrection of the widow's son (17:17-24)

Living in obedience to the Word of God does not mean that life is trouble-free. The widow and Elijah soon discovered this to be true. The bin of flour and the jar of oil continued to produce just as God had promised, but suddenly the widow's son became so ill that he died (17:17).

This was a very bizarre twist. The young man's survival was implicit in the promise of the Lord to sustain the woman and her son by multiplying their food (17:13-14). The promise to sustain them with the meal and the oil included the phrase **'until the day the LORD sends rain on the earth'** (17:14), but the drought had not ended and yet one of those to whom the promise was given had died.

The widow saw the strange incongruity of it all. Had the Lord promised to sustain her and her son only to drive their hopes up so that he could suddenly dash them to the ground? Had the Lord suddenly remembered some evil in her past that now caused him to forget about his promise? (17:18).

But Elijah, knowing that God never fails to keep his promises, refused to take this young man's death as final. As far as he was concerned, the death of the boy did not in any way negate or nullify the promise of God. Perhaps he thought of Abraham taking Isaac up the mountain to sacrifice him.

Abraham did not know whether he would actually have to offer up his son, but he did know that Isaac had to live even if it meant God raising him from the dead. Abraham knew this because he had a promise from God that could not be fulfilled except through Isaac (Gen. 17:19-21; Heb. 11:17,19).

Believing that he also had from God a promise that the widow's son would be sustained until the drought ended, Elijah took action. He carried the child to the upper room where he was staying, placed him on his own bed, and began to pray (17:19-20). This was no ordinary, nonchalant prayer. It must be called fervent prayer because Elijah **'cried out to the Lord'** (17:20) and **'stretched himself out on the child'** (17:21) as if he would impart his very life to him if he could.

It was a prayer full of faith because Elijah reasoned with God and pleaded his promise before him: **'O Lord my God, have you also brought tragedy on the widow with whom I lodge, by killing her son?'** (17:20). This amounted to Elijah saying: 'Lord, you can't allow this. You have made a promise to sustain this widow and her son and you must honour your promise. Your honour and glory are at stake here.'[1]

Elijah's prayer must also be characterized as tenacious and persevering. Not once, not twice, but three times he stretched himself out on the child, praying with each 'stretch'. Perhaps we do not 'stretch' the meaning too far if we allow Elijah's stretching to make us think of the Lord stretching out on the cross that he might provide eternal life for his people.

We do not understand prayer, but God does. It is one of the great means that he has appointed to accomplish his purpose, and he delights in it. Because he delights in it, he would have us take it seriously, and he teaches us to take it seriously by laying before us in the Scriptures examples of fervent, believing and persevering prayer.

God honoured this type of prayer from Elijah by raising the widow's son from the dead (17:22), a staggering proof of God's reality that confirmed the faith of the widow (17:24).

Elijah in Baal's homeland

Elijah's time at the widow's house should not be considered a strange interlude in the account of the prophet's struggle with Baal, but rather an integral part of it. It was not by accident that the widow lived in Zarephath, which was very near Sidon, and Sidon was part of Phoenicia, the area where Baal worship was spawned.

By sending Elijah to the widow, the Lord was placing him in Baal's homeland. By placing his prophet there, the Lord was able to demonstrate powerfully, in a wonderful and ironic way, the impotence of Baal and the folly of worshipping him. F. C. Fensham suggests that Elijah's presence in Phoenicia was 'to demonstrate on Phoenician soil, where Baal is worshipped, that Yahweh has power over things in which Baal has failed'.[2]

There in Phoenicia the prophet was the instrument of the Lord to show that it was the Lord, and not Baal, who controlled nature. The widow's meal and oil were multiplied by the Lord. The widow's son was raised from the dead by the Lord. Meanwhile Baal, who would seem to be most powerful in his homeland and on behalf of his own people, was nowhere to be found. He was nowhere to be found because he had no objective existence.

The significance of Elijah's presence in Baal's homeland goes beyond showing the impotence of Baal. It also forcefully teaches the following lessons:

1. The fact that Elijah, who was the embodiment of God's Word at this point, moved from Cherith, where he was secluded, to Zarephath, where he served, shows that God not only sustains his Word, but actively uses it to accomplish his purposes. When it appears that God's cause is lost and his Word has failed, the people of God can always be sure that he sustains his cause and uses his Word in ways that we do not realize.

2. The fact that Elijah was sent out of Israel to a Gentile woman shows that those who possess the Word of God, as Israel did, can be set aside and others brought in. Elijah's presence in Zarephath was a miniature picture of that time when the Gentiles would flood into the church because of the Jews' rejection of Christ (Luke 4:25-26; Rom. 10:19; 11;11).

3. The widow's ready acceptance of Elijah's command to bring him her last bit of food showed her readiness to give God priority instead of her own comfort. The people of Israel, in embracing Baal, had done exactly the opposite. This woman stood, therefore, as a stinging rebuke to Israel for losing their way and inverting their priorities.

4. The raising of the widow's son came as a glorious encouragement to the prophet. There was no need for him to despair over the cause of God in Israel. The same God who could raise a child from the dead could also raise a nation to new spiritual life.

5. The raising of the widow's son provides immense comfort to the children of God in every era. The same God who raised that young man has also promised to raise the bodies of all believers unto eternal glory with himself. The resurrection of Jesus from the dead is the guarantee of the resurrection of all those who belong to him.

How can it be said that these important lessons emerge from Elijah's stay with the widow when no one in Israel was even aware that he was there? We can only say that while Elijah's visit to Zarephath and its lessons may have been lost on those Israelites with whom Elijah was dealing, the account came to be recorded in Scripture, where it serves as a reminder to the people of God in every generation not to give to another the love, worship and service that belong to God.

25.
Three challenges

Please read 1 Kings 18:1-21

The time had come to end the drought, but it was not enough for Elijah to announce its end as he had its beginning (17:1). It was God's design to end it in such a way that Baal would be completely discredited. Elijah therefore set out to confront Ahab with a distinct and definite plan in mind (18:19).

Even the manner in which the prophet confronted Ahab was important. Ahab had been searching high and low for Elijah for **'many days'** (18:1) by sending deputies into the surrounding nations (18:10). While they searched Ahab no doubt entertained images of Elijah being brought into his presence and thrust down before him. How delightful it would be for him to force out of Elijah the prophetic word that would end the drought before despatching the prophet into the next life!

But the Lord would never allow Ahab the satisfaction of finding Elijah. When the prophet finally appeared it would not be on Ahab's terms, but on God's. God, who had made Elijah the representative of his Word, would not have the prophet answering the summons of the king who had so despised that Word. Instead it would be Ahab who answered the summons of that Word. Furthermore, the summons of the Word would be delivered through none other than a faint-hearted believer, Obadiah.

The challenge to Obadiah (18:1-16)

Obadiah, the administrator or overseer of Ahab's household (18:3), was out searching for water (18:5), when Elijah suddenly appeared. It is a remarkable commentary on Ahab's character that he had divided the land between himself and Obadiah because he was concerned about the survival of his horses and mules (18:5). In the midst of a dying people, he focused on his livestock! Meanwhile he certainly ought to have known from the law of Moses that it was his idolatrous ways that had caused the drought (Deut. 28:15-18,22-24). But his heart was so hard that he would rather search for a few remaining trickles of water than break with his sin.

Obadiah is one of the great enigmas of the Bible. On one hand, he **'feared the LORD greatly'** and evidenced that fear by hiding one hundred prophets of the Lord from Jezebel and by providing for them (18:3-4). On the other hand, Obadiah was evidently a trusted servant of the vile Ahab. How could a genuine saint of God be so closely associated with such a wicked man?

One would have expected that Obadiah would have been glad to see Elijah. Only the appearance of the prophet could bring to an end the unbearable suffering caused by the drought. Only the appearance of the prophet could finally bring clarity to a nation torn between the impossible synthesis between Baal and God.

But Obadiah was not happy to see Elijah at all because the prophet insisted on pressing him into service (18:8). Immediately Obadiah lodged his protest. Ahab would most certainly kill him! Ahab had conducted an extensive search for the prophet. If Obadiah were suddenly to announce Elijah's presence the king might think he had known his whereabouts all along. Or, given the Lord's ability to make Elijah disappear as quickly as he appeared, Obadiah feared he would be gone when Ahab arrived (18:12). In either case, Obadiah was convinced his doom was sealed!

Obadiah tried to dissuade Elijah from using him. He reminded the prophet of what he had secretly done in the cause of the Lord (18:13), but Elijah was undeterred. He would present himself to Ahab that very day (18:15) and Obadiah was to be the means to this end. When Obadiah saw that Elijah would not budge, he went, perhaps with a sigh of resignation, to meet Ahab.

Why did Elijah consider it to be so important to include Obadiah in his plans? The prophet was, as we have noted, the representative of the Word of God, and Obadiah the representative of the believing remnant in Israel. In issuing his summons to Ahab through Obadiah, the Word of God was pressing the believing remnant into service. Secret discipleship would not avail in the struggle against Baal!

The challenge to Ahab (18:17-19)

Soon after the trembling Obadiah went to deliver Elijah's message, the blustery Ahab appeared. The first words out of his mouth showed the condition of his heart: **'Is that you, O troubler of Israel?'** (18:17).

Ahab was correct on one point: there was trouble in Israel. But it was he, not the prophet, who was the source of it, and Elijah let him know that in no uncertain terms. It was the king's responsibility to lead the nation to be true to her covenant with God. Covenant faithfulness was the way to prosperity for the nation. But Ahab and his father before him had launched an all-out offensive against covenant faithfulness, and the blessing it would bring, by going after Baal (18:18).

The folly of Ahab's idolatry was already apparent. Even though he was hailed as the storm-god, Baal had been unable to break the drought announced by Elijah. Even with this abundant evidence in place, Elijah proposed something further. The hardness of Ahab's heart was such that yet more evidence of Baal's impotence was needed — evidence that was so unspeakably clear that it could not be denied or explained away. With this in mind, Elijah challenged Ahab to assemble the entire nation, the 450 prophets of Baal and the 400 prophets of Asherah, a fertility goddess who was considered to be the mother of Baal. While Elijah did not go into detail about his plans, Ahab certainly had to realize that his god was being offered the opportunity to demonstrate decisively that he was real and to lay to rest the question of whether he should be worshipped in Israel. Such an opportunity could not be ignored, and Ahab readily complied with the prophet's demand (18:19-20).

The challenge to the people (18:20-21)

We cannot say how many people assembled on the day of meeting on Mt Carmel. Elijah's phrase **'all Israel'** (18:19) should not be taken to mean that every single person in Israel was present. We should allow Elijah to speak in the same way that we ourselves often do. When we say, 'Everyone is going to the new restaurant,' we do not mean to suggest that all without exception are going there, but rather a large number.

Neither can we say with what attitude, or spirit, the people of Israel came. Many probably came with a good measure of hostility towards the prophet. Israel had suffered much because of the drought, and a large part of the population would undoubtedly have sided with Ahab in blaming Elijah (18:17).

It may be that many of the people came as mere spectators to see how the dramatic confrontation between the prophets of Baal and Elijah would unfold. There may very well have been considerable excitement and eagerness as they gathered.

If indeed the people came to Mt Carmel with the notion that they were bystanders in the conflict, they were in for a shock. Elijah, dispensing with the pleasantries, confronted them with these words: **'How long will you falter between two opinions? If the LORD is God, follow him; but if Baal, follow him'** (18:21).

It is certainly true that Ahab and Jezebel were primarily responsible for the Baal worship in Israel, but the people were not without responsibility. Baal worship could not have flourished in an atmosphere of total devotion to the Lord, but the people had failed to give that total devotion. Instead of standing firmly against Baal, they had faltered **'between two opinions'**. The word **'falter'** (18:21) can be translated 'limp'. The situation called for them to move quickly and decisively to declare their allegiance to God, but they had limped along.

In other words, the people had joined their king in thinking that a synthesis between Baal and God could be achieved. They had assured themselves that it was not necessary for them to make a choice between Baal and God, that they could in fact worship both without doing violence to either. There is no difficulty in understanding why they found this position so appealing. On one hand, they wanted to be true to the God of their fathers, but, on the other hand, they wanted to be in step with their neighbours who also worshipped Baal. We may also rest assured that the sexual rites which were part and parcel of Baal worship were no small part of its attraction.

The perfect solution, as far as the people were concerned, was to worship both. They would attribute the fertility of the land to Baal and the rest of life to God. Their synthesis did not take into account the fact that Baal and God were claiming the same territory; that is, each claimed exclusive control of the weather and fertility. Both could not be right.

The drought announced by Elijah must have shaken the easy-going complacency of the people, but they were still unwilling to let go of the Baal worship that pandered to their flesh.

Elijah framed the issue in such a way that the people had to agree in principle that their attempted synthesis was impossible (18:22-24).

The messages of the three challenges

Each of the three meetings described in these verses speaks to God's people today.

The message of the challenge to Obadiah

The prophet's summons to Obadiah reminds us that God has placed his people in a spiritual warfare, and we are all called to be actively engaged. As the Word of God called Obadiah to service, so it calls us to stand firm against Satan and to be faithful to our God.

The message of the challenge to Ahab

Elijah's challenge to Ahab reminds us to insist boldly that any people who flaunt God's laws throw the door of their lives wide open to trouble. Scripture says, 'Righteousness exalts a nation, but sin is a reproach to any people' (Prov. 14:34).

We must also insist that those who stand for God's truth do not pose a threat to society, but rather those who rebel against that truth.

The message of the challenge to the people

Elijah's challenge to the people of Israel is perfectly summarized in these words from Jesus: 'No one can serve two masters; for either he will hate the one and love the other, or else he will be loyal to the one and despise the other. You cannot serve God and mammon' (Matt. 6:24).

26.
Elijah confronts the prophets of Baal

Please read 1 Kings 18:22-40

The prophets of Baal may well have grinned from ear to ear when they heard Elijah's proposition. They were to prepare a bull for sacrifice and Elijah would do the same. The god who sent fire to consume the sacrifice would be acknowledged as God (18:23-24). Elijah had played right into their hands. Fire was Baal's speciality. He was the storm-god who sent the lightning and the rain.

Or perhaps Baal's prophets did not welcome this challenge at all. They may have found themselves wondering how Baal could send fire when for more than three years he had not been able to produce rain. Even if they were uncertain as to whether Baal could, or would, send fire, they still had to accept Elijah's challenge. To refuse would have been tantamount to acknowledging that their god was a sham.

The prophets of Baal pray for fire (18:25-29)

Whatever their frame of mind, the Baal-worshippers set to work. They chose their bull and prepared it for sacrifice, but put no wood under it. Then they began to pray, **'O Baal, hear us!'** (18:26). Fervently and urgently they prayed. They demonstrated their emotional fervour by leaping around the altar as they prayed, but it was all to no avail. The account puts it succinctly and forcefully: **'But there was no voice; no one answered'** (18:26).

There was no answer because Baal was not there, and he was not there because he was not real. He was the result of men's attempt to construct a god to suit themselves. A person can get by with a make-believe god until he needs a real answer. Then he must have the real God.

When the prophets of Baal began their praying in the morning, Elijah was content to leave them alone. But at noon he began to mock them. Why were they not receiving the answer they so desperately desired? Could it be that they were not calling loud enough? Perhaps Baal was so preoccupied with other matters that he had not heard them. Maybe he was meditating, on a journey, or even sleeping (18:27). If any of these were the case, the solution was for them to cry even louder.

Under the lash of Elijah's taunting, the Baal-worshippers prayed still louder (18:28). They even sought to evoke Baal's pity by cutting themselves. Still there was no answer, no fire. Caked with their own blood, hoarse from their shouting and exhausted from their exertions, these false prophets of the false god Baal came to the evening hours with nothing to show for their efforts. The Bible closes the lid on their sorry attempts by again calling attention to the total silence that followed their prayers: **'But there was no voice; no one answered, no one paid attention'** (18:29).

Elijah prays for fire (18:30-40)

Now it was Elijah's turn. A quiet calm seems to have settled on the assembly when Elijah asked the people to come near to him (18:30). That calm must have been very welcome indeed after a day of listening to the shrieking of the Baal-worshippers and watching their strange gyrations. Some think Elijah wanted the people to draw very near so they would be convinced that there was no trickery involved in what he was about to do. It is more likely that he wanted them near so that what they heard and saw would make an even more lasting impression upon them.

The altar he repaired (18:30-32)

Elijah first turned his attention to repairing an old altar of the Lord. Before the temple in Jerusalem was built, the people of God built several altars for sacrifice and worship throughout the land. These altars were not to be used after the completion of the temple, but now the kingdom was divided and the people of Israel no longer enjoyed access to the temple in Jerusalem. For them to worship the Lord, it was necessary for them once again to make use of these altars. One of them was there on Mt Carmel. Its state of disrepair may reflect the destructive zeal of Jezebel to destroy such altars (19:10), the apathy of the people of God to maintain the worship of God, or both.

It was this altar on Mt Carmel that the prophet rebuilt in the sight of all the people. It is significant that he used twelve stones in the process. Every Israelite understood what that number represented. The kingdom of Israel consisted of ten tribes and the kingdom of Judah two. But those twelve tribes were all part of one kingdom before the people went after idols. Its division was a testimony to the havoc sin creates, and the twelve stones Elijah used showed the unity that could have been theirs had it not been for idolatry. Those stones also represented the unity that God would have renewed if they had been willing to turn from their idols.

The sacrifice he prepared (18:33)

After repairing the altar, Elijah turned his attention to placing the sacrifice upon it. It is noteworthy that Elijah did not just pray for rain. Israel was in dire need of rain, but Elijah was seeking fire to consume his sacrifice. Why did he focus on fire when the need was for rain? Elijah knew the drought was not Israel's primary problem but rather the result of it. Idolatry was the real problem in Israel, and the way to solve the drought problem was to confess the sin problem. The sacrificing of animals was the means God had appointed for dealing with sin. When someone brought a sacrifice to God, he was affirming that he himself was worthy of death because of his sins and was offering the animal as his substitute.

The water he poured (18:33-34)

After preparing his sacrifice, Elijah did something very shocking indeed. The people must have wondered what he was about to do when they saw him dig a trench around the altar. His intention became clear when he commanded that four pots full of water be poured on the sacrifice. That pouring was followed by a second and a third (18:34). The twelve pots of water enabled Elijah to preach once again to the people about God's will for their nation.

Some have wondered how Elijah came to have this water after a prolonged drought. In all likelihood, he had arranged for it to be brought up from the Mediterranean Sea, which was very near Mt Carmel.

After the third and final emptying of the four pots, the sacrifice was fully drenched and water was standing in the trench Elijah had dug (18:35).

Why did Elijah go to all this effort to pour so much water on his sacrifice? His purpose in doing so was to make his sacrifice incapable of being burned by mere human means. If such a soaked sacrifice was to burn there could be no doubt about the origin of the fire! It would not be Elijah but God!

The church of today would do well to stop seeking programmes of dry tinder that are calculated to catch fire easily and win a great following, and give herself instead to pouring water on her own abilities. Only when the people of God shut themselves up to the Lord do they see his might on their behalf.

The prayer he prayed (18:36-38)

With all the preliminaries out of the way, the man of God turned his attention to prayer. It is likely that he deliberately chose the time for this prayer to coincide with the evening sacrifice in Jerusalem (18:36). By so doing, he gave the people yet another reminder of the unity that had been destroyed by sin and could be restored by God.

Elijah's prayer was totally unlike those of the Baal-worshippers. There was no great commotion here, no ranting or raving. The prophet's was primarily a prayer for God to glorify himself by giving indisputable confirmation to the people that he was indeed God. It was a prayer of unwavering faith. Elijah knew the Lord had on previous occasions sent fire from heaven to bear witness to his reality (Lev. 9:24; Judg. 6:17,21; 1 Chr. 21:26). It was also a prayer of intensity as Elijah pleaded with the Lord to hear him (18:37). The Lord did hear him. The fire of the Lord fell from heaven, consumed Elijah's sacrifice and even licked up the water that was in the trench (18:38).

Practical truths

The following applications may be drawn from Elijah's contest with the prophets of Baal:

1. The fact that a religion is popular does not mean it is of God. The prophets of Baal far outnumbered Elijah on this occasion, but he alone was in touch with the true God. In this day in which public opinion polls abound, we do well to remember that living according to God's revealed truth is what counts.

2. The fact that religious activities move the emotions does not mean they are of God. The Baal-worshippers were far more emotional than Elijah, but they were totally mistaken. The fact that true religion can and does move the emotions does not mean that every religion that stirs the emotions is true.

3. True praying is laying hold of God's promises and pleading them before him with hearts that are aflame with the desire for his name to be glorified.

4. Elijah's sacrifice points us to the one whom all the animal sacrifices of the Old Testament were intended to anticipate, Jesus Christ. On the cross, he offered himself as a sacrifice to God. The animal sacrifices had no power actually to deal with sin, but on the cross Christ actually made atonement for the sins of his people. He there received the wrath of God in their stead, and, in receiving it, released them from it for ever.

27.
The aftermath of Mt Carmel

Please read 1 Kings 18:39 - 19:3

The Bible often associates mountains with exhilarating spiritual experiences.

It was on Mount Moriah that the gospel was preached to Abraham. A ram caught in a thicket became the substitute sacrifice for Abraham's son Isaac. Substitution of the innocent for the guilty is the very essence of the gospel!

Mount Sinai was the place where Moses encountered the Lord in such a way that his face glistened with glory.

On Mount Tabor, as tradition has it, three of Jesus' disciples, Peter, James and John, saw him take on a heavenly appearance. The sight was so glorious that Simon Peter suggested that they build booths so they could dwell there for a while (Mark 9:5).

Mt Carmel was, as we have been noting, the site of Elijah's greatest spiritual experience.

But the Bible is not just a book of mountain-tops. It is also a book of valleys, spiritual valleys in which the soul often feels perplexed and sometimes in deep despair. Moses came down from Mt Sinai only to be confronted with the frightful idolatry of his people (Exod. 32:15-19). Peter, James and John descended from Mount Tabor to find their fellow-disciples vainly trying to help a man with a demon-possessed son (Mark 9:14-18).

No one has ever descended from a mountain into the depths more rapidly than Elijah. No one has ever fallen so far so fast as he. In the closing verses of chapter 18 he is standing on the mountain of victory. As he basked in the warm glow of that victory, he may very well have allowed himself to think that the struggle against Baal was finally over. In the opening verses of chapter 19 all suddenly and drastically changes. Elijah topples from the mountain of victory to the valley of despair. We now trace the prophet's downward slide from that glad moment when the people acknowledged the Lord to that sad moment when he fled from Jezebel.

The people acknowledge the Lord (18:39)

Elijah had plainly stipulated that the God who answered by fire would be acknowledged as God, and there could be no doubt about what had happened. Elijah had prayed and the Lord had answered by fire. The people, having agreed with Elijah's stipulation, now had no choice but to cry, **'The Lord, he is God! The Lord, he is God.'**

We cannot help but wonder how the people could confess the Lord in such a seemingly sincere way without anything really changing in Israel. It was not the first time people professed something that they did not really believe. The forefathers of Elijah's generation were released from bondage in Egypt with Pharaoh and his people sending them out of the land 'in haste' (Exod. 12:33). But Israel was no sooner out of the land than Pharaoh said, 'Why have we done this, that we have let Israel go from serving us?' (Exod. 14:5).

The impression of awe and fear that Pharaoh felt when Israel's God caused the first-born of Egypt to die (Exod. 12:29-30) melted away when he lost some of his comforts. It is likely that much the same happened with Elijah's generation.

The impression of awe that was made by the fire from heaven soon vanished when the people stopped to weigh the fleshly comforts that were part and parcel of Baal-worship.

Elijah executes the prophets of Baal (18:40)

While the people were still caught up in the euphoria of the moment, Elijah ordered that the prophets of Baal be seized and put to death. This detail inevitably creates consternation. How could Elijah claim that his religion was superior to that of the Baal-worshippers when he commanded their execution? Was this act due to his failing to accurately understand and reflect the nature of the God he professed to serve?

Although it offends our modern sensibilities, the truth is that Elijah commanded the execution of the false prophets out of fidelity to the law that God himself had given to Israel (Deut. 13:1-5; 17:2-7).

Furthermore, it is very likely that these prophets had carried out Jezebel's massacre of the prophets of the Lord (18:4, 13). If so, it was only just for these men to pay with their own lives for the lives they had taken.

Elijah prays for rain (18:41-45)

With the prophets of Baal out of the way, Elijah told Ahab to eat and drink, **'for there is the sound of abundance of rain'** (18:41). In other words, he called for Ahab to begin celebrating because the sorely needed rain was on the way. How did Elijah know this? God had stated in the law that he would send rain upon his people when they turned back to him from their idols (Deut. 11:13-17). The temporary nature of the positive response of the people would not keep God from being gracious to them. God is faithful even when his people fail to be. In addition to this, Elijah had also received a direct and immediate promise from the Lord that he was about to send rain (18:1).

Elijah was right, then, to tell Ahab to celebrate, but he does not join in the celebration. Instead he turns his attention again to prayer. This time he prays not for fire, but for rain.

There is a mystery here. Elijah is so certain of rain that he tells Ahab to celebrate, but yet he prays. Why did Elijah find it necessary to pray for rain if it was already on the way? To put it another way, why is it necessary to pray for those things that God has already promised? To us praying for what has been promised seems to be pointless, but God views it differently. Prayer is the means by which God has chosen to bestow what he has promised. Therefore, if we desire the end, what God has promised, we must make use of the means he has appointed, prayer.

Elijah would not allow the promise of rain to make him casual in prayer. He showed his humility by bowing down **'on the ground'**, and by putting his face **'between his knees'** (18:42). This was real praying. Elijah was not merely going through the motions. He was laying hold of the promise of God with prayer that was not only humble but fervent.

It was persistent praying as well. The prophet sent his servant to look towards the sea for an indication of rain and received the report that there was nothing. Undeterred, the prophet sent the servant again and again until he saw **'a cloud, as small as a man's hand, rising out of the sea!'** (18:44).

Elijah knew he had his answer. God's promise was like a cord connecting heaven and earth, and through prayer he had pulled on the cord and brought the promise down. There would now be such an abundance of rain that it was necessary for Ahab to get on his way to Jezreel before the rain stopped him (18:44).

Elijah runs in triumph before Ahab (18:46)

As Ahab set out for Jezreel, sixteen miles away, Elijah began to run before his chariot and continued to do so until the two arrived at the gate of Jezreel. How are we to explain this? We do not have to come up with an explanation because the author himself says, **'Then the hand of the LORD came upon Elijah...'**

If we believe that God sent fire from heaven to consume Elijah's sacrifice, we should have no difficulty in believing that the same God could give Elijah strength to outdistance a chariot for sixteen miles. On the other hand, if we do not believe God sent fire from heaven or gave Elijah unusual strength for running, we do not believe the God of the Bible. The God who can make a donkey talk (Num. 22:28-30) can make a prophet run!

In our concern to explain how Elijah was capable of all this running, we often lose sight of an even larger question, namely, the Lord's purpose in causing his prophet to do this. Is it not likely that the Lord did this to teach Ahab a much-needed lesson? The prophet, as we have noted throughout, was the representative of the Word of God, and it was in that capacity that he ran before the king. If Ahab desired to have the blessing of God upon him and to avoid catastrophes such as the drought, he must learn to follow God's Word with his heart and mind, even as he followed Elijah in his chariot. It was his responsibility as King of Israel to follow that Word himself and to lead his nation to follow it as well. Ahab had failed miserably up to this point and would tragically continue to do so.

Elijah runs in fear from Jezebel (19:1-3)

The greatness of Elijah's fear

How swiftly things can change for the saint of God! For six-teen miles Elijah ran in triumph before Ahab's chariot. The next thing we know, he is running again. This time there is no triumph but only fear. The author says the prophet **'ran for his life'** (19:3). Little fear would have caused Elijah to have fled only a short distance. But his was not little fear, so he ran and ran and ran. Elijah ran from Jezreel, situated in the centre of Israel, all the way into the neighbouring kingdom of Judah. He was not even content to get out of Israel. Once in Judah he continued his journey to Beersheba, which was at the southernmost edge of the kingdom and 130 miles from Jezreel. There he left his servant (19:3), whom we meet for the first time. We know nothing about this man. Since Elijah was most certainly alone at Cherith and Zarephath, we can only assume that he engaged this servant immediately before his meeting with the prophets of Baal on Mt Carmel. Perhaps upon his engagement, the servant was sent to Jezreel, where he was to meet Elijah after the Mt Carmel episode.

The reason for Elijah's fear

What was it that caused Elijah to shift so abruptly from run-ning in triumph to running in fear? It was none other than the wicked Jezebel. When Ahab reported to her the day's events and the execution of her prophets, she flew into a rage and swore to kill Elijah (19:1-2).

A threat from one woman should not have cowered one who had stood fearlessly before hundreds of false proph-ets, but it did, and we are left wondering why. Did Elijah run because he was surprised by Jezebel's outburst? Did he accompany Ahab to Jezreel with the expectation that the victory was now assured and Baal-worship would be banished from the land? That would seem to be a legitimate hope since Jezebel's religion had been so totally discredited and the people had so vigorously cried, 'The LORD, he is God! The LORD, he is God!' (18:39).

If Elijah indeed nurtured such a hope, he seriously underestimated the wicked Jezebel. Had her commitment to Baal been based on evidence, it would have been realistic to expect her to abandon Baal. But her devotion to Baal was never a matter of evidence. It was rather a matter of her essentially saying, 'I worship Baal because it makes me feel good.'

Many Christians persist in thinking that all we must do to bring sinners to Christ is to present the evidence for him. If we only win the argument, the thinking goes, we can expect opposition to crumble and our gospel to be embraced. This analysis fails to see the nature of the opposition. People today do not merely reject the gospel because they regard it as being untrue. They reject it because they do not want it to be true. They reject it so they may give themselves to views that make them feel good and place no demands upon them.

Elijah ran from Jezebel because he desperately wanted the struggle with Baal to be over, and Jezebel's response made it clear that it was not. Not only was the struggle not over; the outcome of it must now have seemed to the prophet to be in doubt.

28.
Elijah renewed and recommissioned

Please read 1 Kings 19:4-21

The story of Elijah would be sad indeed if it ended with the prophet running in terror from Jezebel, but God would not let it end in such a way. He would not let the prophet who strode so boldly onto the stage of history run from it in cowardly fear and defeat. The verses to which we now come show us how the Lord took his prophet in hand.

This account oozes grace. The Lord could have been very stern with his prophet. He could have resoundingly rebuked him and discharged him from the field of service. But the Lord dealt very tenderly with Elijah and sent him back into service. This nineteenth chapter of 1 Kings, which begins in such despondency and despair, ends in triumph because of the grace of God.

Elijah journeys to Mt Horeb (19:4-8)

The prophet prays to die (19:4)

With his servant, who must have been exhausted by the fevered journey, left behind in Beersheba, Elijah went a day's journey into the wilderness. There he sat down under **'a broom tree'**, which the *MacArthur Study Bible* describes as: 'A desert bush that grew to a height of 10 ft. It had slender branches featuring small leaves and fragrant blossoms.'[1]

Under this tree Elijah finally gave expression to the despair that had been churning within him. There he prayed, **'It is enough! Now, Lord, take my life, for I am no better than my fathers!'** (19:4). The man who was afraid of dying by Jezebel's hand now prays to die by the Lord's hand! Elijah was at his lowest ebb. As far as he was concerned, the battle was over, and it was time for him, the Lord's soldier in this battle, to be discharged from service. The flame of faith that burned so brightly at the beginning was now barely flickering.

To whom was the prophet referring when he said, 'I am no better than my fathers!'? (19:4). It is significant that he was there in the very wilderness in which so many of his forefathers had died. The Israelites whom Moses led out of Egypt had turned back in unbelief from the border of Canaan and had died in the wilderness as God raised up a new generation (Num. 14:28-29; 26:64-65). They had failed to do what God had called them to do, and Elijah in that same wilderness was convinced that he had also failed and should therefore share the same fate as they.

The prophet receives a visit from an angel (19:5-7)

How the tender grace of the Lord shines in these verses! The Lord did not answer Elijah's prayer (we should be thankful the Lord does not give us everything we ask for). Neither did the Lord sternly rebuke his prophet. Instead he sent an angel to feed him. This was the third time Elijah was miraculously fed, each time in a different way, and each way designed to bolster Elijah's faith. The ravens at Cherith brought food to Elijah that they would normally have eaten themselves, and in doing so affirmed for the prophet that the Lord, not Baal, was truly the God of nature. The meal and oil at the widow's house in Zarephath affirmed for Elijah that God sustains his cause and uses his Word even when all appears to be lost, as it did in Israel at that time.

The Lord's use of the angel on this occasion may have been intended to speak to Elijah in two ways. First, the angel, as one of the heavenly host, was an indication that the struggle against Baal was not as hopeless as it appeared. The Lord, who is sovereign over the countless angels who carry out his commands, was sovereign over Jezebel and Baal. He does not express his sovereignty in the ways that his people would often choose, but while his ways are mysterious, his sovereignty assures that his purposes will finally be achieved and his cause will finally prevail.

The second way in which the angel spoke to Elijah was on the matter of obedience. The angel was there in the presence of Elijah because the Lord had despatched him to the prophet and the angel had obeyed. What a contrast this was with Elijah himself, who had taken his long journey without a command from the Lord to do so!

The prophet completes his journey (19:8)

After receiving two rounds of sustenance from the angel, Elijah continued his journey to Mt Horeb, which is another name for Mt Sinai. This mountain was located about 200 miles south of Beersheba, and should have taken Elijah less than half the forty days and nights that he used to journey there. We may rest assured that the journey took Elijah so long because the Lord, with whom there are no insignificant details, intended that it should take his prophet exactly forty days and forty nights.

The significance of the number forty would not have been lost on the prophet. He was travelling in the same wilderness in which the exodus generation had wandered and died. As he walked past their graves he would be compelled to connect their experience with his own. The cause of God appeared to have failed when that generation refused to enter the land of Canaan, but it did not fail. It took forty years, but God raised up a new generation to whom he gave the land of Canaan, as he had promised, and the cause of God went on. The graves in the wilderness must have been a powerful testimony to Elijah not to give up on God when he seems to have been utterly defeated.

Elijah on Mt Horeb (19:9-18)

We cannot be sure, but it would seem to be a safe guess that Elijah had Mt Horeb in mind as his final destination from the very beginning of his flight. Why did he desire to go there? As far as he was concerned, Mt Horeb was where it had all begun. That was where the Lord had established his covenant with the people of Israel after their deliverance from Egypt. There they had proclaimed their eagerness to be faithful to the Lord (Exod. 24:1-8). Elijah now considered it all to be over. He was going back to Mt Horeb, the place of the beginning, to report to the Lord that it had all ended. At Mt Horeb the Lord had had a whole nation. Now the Lord was down to one solitary prophet. The whole enterprise had gone down the drain! The covenant was forsaken. The altars of the Lord had been torn down. The prophets of the Lord had been eliminated. With all his zeal, Elijah had not been able to stem the tide (19:10).

Elijah came to Mt Horeb with removal on his mind, his removal from the battlefield. But it was renewal, not removal, that the Lord had in mind. The Lord went about this matter of renewing his prophet by creating a strong wind, an earthquake and a fire, but the Lord was not in these things (19:11-12). After these powerful forces were spent, the Lord spoke to Elijah in **'a still small voice'** (19:12).

What did it all mean? We have a tendency to think that the wind, the earthquake and the fire were somehow opposed to God because he was not in them. The truth is, however, that while God was not in them, he did produce them as he **'passed by'**. They were, therefore, his instruments. By producing these things the Lord was showing Elijah that he, the Lord, was indeed adequate for the struggle. He who can command the wind, earthquake and fire does not lack for instruments. In fact he was about to introduce into the struggle against Baal some mighty instruments: Hazael, Jehu and Elisha (19:15-17).

But while the Lord is more than adequate for the struggle, he himself is above the struggle. The wind, earthquake and fire revealed the former, while the still small voice revealed the latter. The Lord is capable of using turbulence to accomplish his purposes, but he never experiences turbulence.

Elijah came to Mount Horeb in a fit of turbulence, convinced that all was lost, but the Lord did not share his turbulence. While all seemed hopeless to Elijah, the Lord had everything under control. Elijah was so filled with turbulence that he thought he alone was left, but the Lord in his sovereign control had reserved for himself 7,000 faithful ones (19:18). Elijah faltered when he forgot his place, which was faithfully obeying the orders of his Lord, and inserted himself into the Lord's place, which was to sustain his own cause. The prophet was not wrong to have a burden for the cause of the Lord. He was wrong to allow that burden to drive him to despair. There was no need for despair because the Lord whom Elijah served was both adequate for the struggle and above the struggle.

Elijah leaves Mount Horeb (19:19-21)

God did not grant the revelation of Mount Horeb so Elijah could merely sit back and enjoy it. It was designed to pull the prophet back from the desire for discharge and to rekindle his desire for service. It worked. In leaving Mount Horeb to seek Elisha, the prophet was going back to what had been his pattern prior to his flight, that is, promptly obeying the Lord's commands. He was now content to do what he had been called to do with the confidence that God could and would sustain his own cause.

Elijah found Elisha ploughing with twelve yoke of oxen (19:19). Without saying a word, Elijah threw his mantle around the young man's shoulders (evidently the formal anointing was to come later).

Elisha understood the significance of that act. Elijah was calling him to be his successor in the prophetic office. This call represented a radical change for Elisha. He would not have been ploughing with twelve yoke of oxen if his father had not been a very wealthy man. And now Elijah had called him to break with that life and to accept the rigours and hardship of being a prophet. Some degree of hesitation would have been understandable, but Elisha did not hesitate. He would go home to bid farewell to his father and mother and join Elijah. Some suggest Elijah's response, **'Go back again, for what have I done to you'** (19:20) might be better translated, 'Go, but remember what I have done to you.'

Some have wondered why it was permissible for Elisha to bid farewell to his parents, but not permissible for the young man Jesus would meet centuries later to do the same. Jesus responded to his request by saying, 'No one, having put his hand to the plough, and looking back, is fit for the kingdom of God' (Luke 9:62).

The answer to this dilemma lies in the men themselves. Elisha's request came from a heart that was anxious to make a radical break with his lifestyle and follow Elijah. He proved this by slaughtering one of his teams of oxen and cooking them on a fire made from their equipment (19:21). The man with whom Jesus dealt was different. His request came, not from an eagerness to follow Jesus, but rather from a reluctance to do so. His desire to go home was not so that he could make a decisive break from his parents and follow Jesus, but rather to further delay such decisive action.

We should come away from the renewal of Elijah with profound appreciation for the God of grace who never lets his people go. When they run from the field of service, he runs after them, finds them and restores them. We have only to look at another prophet, Jonah, to see the truth of this.

We should also be profoundly grateful for that one servant of God who never ran from the field of service. Although the Lord Jesus Christ was 'in all points tempted as we are' (Heb. 4:15), he never wavered in his commitment to the work assigned to him by the Father, but steadily pursued it until he was able to cry, 'It is finished!' (John 19:30).

29.
Ahab defeats the Syrians

Please read 1 Kings 20:1-22

David, Israel's second and greatest king, grew up as a shepherd boy. He did not cease to be a shepherd when he became king. He just traded his lambs and ewes for people. David was a true shepherd for the nation of Israel. He protected her from her enemies, he nurtured her faith and cared for her oppressed.

Ahab could have learned much from David, but he refused to do so. In this chapter he had ample opportunity to be a true shepherd for his people, but he failed. The essential ingredient for Ahab to be a true shepherd of his people was fidelity to the Word of God.

The next three chapters of 1 Kings focus our attention even more narrowly on Ahab and his attitude to the Word of God. Ronald S. Wallace says, 'The purpose of the next chapters of the book of Kings is to show how the tension between Ahab and the prophets round Elijah revived and grew; and how; finally, he met his death by ignoring and defying the word they proclaimed.'[1] A little later Wallace notes: 'These chapters show how after Carmel the chief factor determining the fate of Ahab was his attitude to the Word of God.'[2]

We should especially note in this chapter the following phrases: **'Suddenly a prophet approached Ahab...'** (20:13). **'And the prophet came to the king of Israel...'** (20:22). **'Then a man of God came and spoke to the king of Israel...'**

(20:28). **'Then the prophet departed and waited for the
king... '** (20:38). Everything in this chapter revolves around
those phrases. Everything is governed by them. It is plain that
Ahab is being confronted with the Word of God and is being
called to obey it. This did not require him to make a leap into
the dark. He had seen the Word of God verified in and through
the ministry of Elijah. In the first part of this chapter, he sees it
verified again.

After a fumbling start, he was able to defeat Syria, but because he lacked a shepherd's heart, he managed to turn the
defeat of Syria into a defeat for Israel. In this chapter, we
focus on Ahab's defeat of Syria and in the next on his defeat of
his own people.

Three phrases emerge from the first half of this chapter to
aptly summarize Ahab's defeat of Syria.

'Now Ben-Hadad the king of Syria ...' (20:1-12)

With this phrase the author abruptly shifts our focus from Israel's internal life to her foreign affairs and from the prophet
Elijah to Ahab. This phrase also brings us with a jolt to a very
serious and dark time for Israel.

The crisis was precipitated by Ben-Hadad of Syria. This
Ben-Hadad was evidently the son of the Ben-Hadad who had
attacked Baasha some years earlier (15:18-19) and had taken
several cities (15:20). The Ben-Hadad of this chapter makes
reference to the cities that his father had taken from Israel
(20:34).

The Ben-Hadad with whom we are concerned here had
been gathering strength for some time, so much so that he had
thirty-two kings in his retinue when he finally laid siege to the
city of Samaria (20:1). Once there he sent a message to Ahab

demanding his silver and gold, his loveliest wives and his children (20:2-3).

Ahab quickly and meekly responded to this demand, saying to Ben-Hadad, **'My lord, O king, just as you say, I and all that I have are yours'** (20:4). Ahab's shameful acquiescence is an indication of how faith in God had ebbed in Israel. One of the covenant blessings God had promised to bestow upon his people was victory over their enemies (Lev. 26:7-8; Deut. 28:7), but this blessing, along with many others, hinged on Israel's faithful obedience to God's laws. Ahab's reign was not a time of faith in God's promises, or of obedience to his law. When faced with Ben-Hadad's demand, Ahab appears to have given no thought at all to turning to God and seeking to renew the nation's covenant with him. He did not see God as the nation's great resource. He merely looked at the stark military reality facing him and complied with the demand.

Ahab's meek response emboldened Ben-Hadad to take things a step further. He sent a second message to Ahab in which he announced that he would send his soldiers into the city to plunder it completely (20:6). This was in addition to that to which Ahab had already agreed (20:5).

This put the cat among the pigeons for Ahab. He called together the elders of Israel and said to them, referring to Ben-Hadad, **'Notice, please, and see how this man seeks trouble...'** (20:7).

The elders advised Ahab to resist this further demand (20:8). When he did so, Ben-Hadad flew into such a rage that he swore that he would reduce Samaria to a pile of dust (20:10). By this time, Ahab was in a rather surly mood himself. He responded to Ben-Hadad's blustery threat by saying, **'Let not the one who puts on his armour boast like the one who takes it off'** (20:11). Several have noted that this amounted to Ahab saying, 'Don't count your chickens before they are hatched.'

The fact that Ben-Hadad and the kings with him received Ahab's message while they were drinking (20:12) suggests that they were supremely confident of victory.

'Suddenly a prophet ...' (20:13-14)

Ahab and his elders may very well have felt a deep sense of resignation to a terrible fate as they agreed to resist Ben-Hadad's demands. Despite his brave words (20:11), Ahab realized his army was no match for the **'great multitude'** (20:13) that surrounded his city. Given that fact, capture, torture and even execution must have loomed before Ahab as very distinct possibilities.

The bleakness of the situation changed very rapidly with the appearance of an unnamed prophet. Ahab, who had once received disconcerting news from the abrupt appearance of Elijah (17:1), now receives cheering news in the same fashion. The Lord, whom Ahab had left out of the equation, now interjects himself into the situation with a question and a promise. He asks Ahab, **'Have you seen all this great multitude?'** He then adds: **'Behold, I will deliver it into your hand today...'** (20:13).

What an unexpected development! Why should the Lord promise victory to the wicked Ahab? Would it not have been a fitting judgement to let the Syrian army make mincemeat of him? We are face to face here with the mystery and majesty of God's grace. Ahab deserved nothing but God's judgement, but God, in amazing patience, gives this detestable king yet another evidence that the Lord God was real and worthy of Israel's and the king's wholehearted devotion.

How good God was to give Ahab this prophetic word! It promised deliverance from certain doom. All of God's people have received such a word, the gospel message, which pronounces deliverance from eternal condemnation through faith in the finished work of the Lord Jesus Christ.

The graciousness of God in speaking to Ahab seems to have been lost on him. He expresses no thanks for it. He was totally unworthy of such a word, but he does not bow and confess his unworthiness and repent of his many wicked deeds. He responds by pressing the prophet for more information. He wants to know how the victory is to be achieved (20:14), and, as yet another token of the stunning grace of God, the prophet answers his enquiries. Ahab himself was to give the signal to advance, and **'the young leaders of the provinces'** (20:14), which may be considered to be something of a special commando unit, were to lead the attack, followed closely by the army (20:19).

'So the Syrians fled ...' (20:15-22)

Ahab, for one bright moment in his otherwise sorry life, did what the Lord told him to do. He mustered his forces and went out at noon. The timing was most propitious as Ben-Hadad and the other kings were more concerned about their drinking than about preparing for battle (20:16).

One cannot help but notice the difference between one king, Ahab, being fortified with the Word of God while the other, Ben-Hadad, fortifies himself with drink. At this point these men are emblematic of two completely different ways of life, both of which are still available to this moment. The one is the life of principled obedience to the Word of God. The other is the life governed by what brings momentary pleasure and gratification. What a shame that it was only during this brief period of time that Ahab exemplified the former!

Ben-Hadad interrupted his drinking long enough to send out a patrol which reported the advance of the young leaders

30.
Ahab defeats Syria — and Israel!

Please read 1 Kings 20:23-43

It is not unusual to hear of someone snatching victory from the jaws of defeat. The last half of 1 Kings 20 confronts us with the sad spectacle of Ahab snatching defeat from the jaws of victory. Ahab managed to turn his second defeat of the Syrians into a defeat for his own nation. He did so by granting clemency to Ben-Hadad. On the surface this could be regarded as a laudable act of compassion on the part of Ahab. In reality it was a flagrant disregard for the honour of God and the welfare of God's people.

The issue (20:23-30)

This passage presents us with much more than political considerations and military manoeuvrings. Through their faulty analysis of their previous defeat, the Syrians moved the issue into a whole different realm: the realm of theology. They blasphemously concluded that their defeat was due to the gods of Israel being **'gods of the hills'** (20:23). They were mistaken on two fronts. First, it was not 'gods', but God, who had given Israel the victory in the previous battle. Israel had indeed worshipped other gods, but these were like the Syrian gods themselves — empty, meaningless nothings. The God who had caused Israel to triumph was, and is, the only true God, who is both the Creator and the Governor of the universe. Secondly, this God was not limited to the hills, as the Syrians were about to learn.

It is crucial to note that an unnamed prophet made sure Ahab was keenly aware of the analysis of the Syrians (20:28). Here is evidence of the sovereignty of God: he had heard what the Syrians had discussed in secret!

The prophet's proclamation of this to Ahab moved the king himself into a new realm. Ronald S. Wallace notes that Ahab was now in the eyes of the prophets '... like a second David entering battle against a boasting pagan Goliath, defiant of the living God! He was the defender and champion of everything that Israel's faith stood for.'[1] Wallace further says, concerning the prophets' view of Ahab in this situation, 'They believed it was impossible for him to fail, and of one thing they were certain that the insult to their God could be purged, and his name vindicated, only through complete and decisive victory involving the death of Ben-hadad who had dared to defy so openly the living God.'[2]

It was indeed impossible for Ahab to fail in this venture because the Lord, through one of his prophets, had graciously promised to give him victory (20:28). This creates something of a dilemma. Why would God give a man like that such a promise? Why would God be so gracious to one as wicked and unworthy as Ahab? In view of the fact that the nation of Israel had largely followed their king into idolatry, we may also ask why God would be so gracious to the nation. Why would God bless his fallen nation in this way?

The answer lies not in Ahab or in Israel, but in the issue we have been examining. The Syrians had challenged God's honour and glory, and God will not abide this. He is jealous for his glory and will not share it with another (Isa. 42:8; 48:11). Ahab and Israel, wicked as they were, were merely God's instruments in this situation to vindicate his honour. God has often used wicked kings and nations to achieve his purpose and to glorify his name. The Jews in exile knew this all too well. They were in captivity because the Lord had used the pagan nation of Babylon as his instrument of judgement upon them.

We may go further and say that by blessing Ahab and Israel in this way, the Lord was giving them further opportunity to come to their senses, repent and turn back to him. The apostle Paul says the goodness of God leads to repentance (Rom. 2:4). To continue on their path to ruin, Israel had to climb over high hills of God's goodness and mountains of his mercy.

How often the church of today is like Israel under Ahab! How often she strays from the Lord and goes after idols! But God continues to be gracious to her. While not approving of his church in a fallen condition, the Lord can still use her to vindicate his name. Sometimes he sends her revival and brings glory to his abounding mercy. Sometimes he allows her to suffer the bitter fruits of her backsliding and thus vindicates the truth of his Word. The church will either go about her task of bringing glory to the Lord, or the Lord will glorify himself in her fallenness. Either way the Lord will have his glory. And when he has completed the task of vindicating his name in this world, the Lord will bring all things down to the end that he has appointed. At that time he will be completely and irreversibly vindicated (Hab. 2:14).

Ben-Hadad's officials also persuaded him to put his new army under the command of military people rather than under the kings who had been with him in the previous battle (20:24). We might say they decided to go with fighters rather than with drunkards (20:16).

Having drawn their conclusions, the Syrian army marched to Aphek (20:26). The exact location of this site is unknown. Howard F. Vos explains: 'There were five Apheks; the battle probably took place either at the one in the plain of Esdraelon or the one east of the Sea of Galilee and commanding the road to Damascus. There are good arguments for both, and it is difficult to determine which is meant.'³

The situation did not look good for Israel. Ben-Hadad had managed once again to field an army that far outnumbered Israel's. Ahab had evidently deployed his army into two companies, and these, in comparison to the Syrian army, looked like **'two little flocks of goats'** (20:27). On the other hand, the Syrian army **'filled the countryside'** (20:27).

The victory (20:29-30)

What the Lord promises he delivers. After the opposing armies faced each other for seven days the battle was joined, and the Syrian army was dealt a crushing defeat. The number of Syrian casualties, 100,000 in one day (20:29), may be symbolic for a very large number. Donald J. Wiseman thinks the phrase translated **'twenty-seven thousand of the men'** who perished when a wall in the city of Aphek fell on them may refer to twenty-seven officers.⁴

Whatever we make of these numbers, it is clear that the Lord gave Israel a resounding victory as he promised.

The compromise (20:31-34)

It is at this point that Ahab turned victory into defeat for Israel. Upon learning Ben-Hadad was still alive, he said, **'He is my brother'** (20:32). Ben-Hadad's servants quickly picked up that word, began referring to Ben-Hadad as Ahab's 'brother', and upon Ahab's request fetched their king (20:33). Ben-Hadad was now quite happy to be the 'brother' of the man whose city he had threatened to reduce to dust (20:10).

Ben-Hadad received a wonderful greeting when he arrived. Ahab indeed treated him as a long-lost brother. He first brought him into his own chariot, as if he were an equal, and then entered into a treaty with him (20:33-34).

What possessed Ahab to treat Ben-Hadad, an inveterate enemy of his people, with such kindness and generosity? Perhaps he wanted to ally himself with the Syrian king as a hedge against the threat posed by the Assyrians, who were rapidly gaining strength.[5] If so, Ahab again showed that he did not understand what he had just witnessed. The Lord had given Israel the victory over the vastly superior Syrian army. It was only reasonable to conclude that the same God could easily protect Israel from Assyria. The priority for Ahab and his people, then, was not making political alliances but rather firmly allying themselves with God by living in obedience to his laws. But Ahab was blind to this conclusion. He preferred to put his trust in a man over whom he had just triumphed rather than in the God who had promised and delivered the triumph.

Why was Ahab's refusal to execute Ben-Hadad such a signal failure? It indicated that Ahab, although he had been informed in advance of the issue at stake, did not see the battle in terms of the honour and glory of the Lord. He saw it, rather, in personal terms. His victory gave him the opportunity to show how wonderfully generous and magnanimous he could be. Everyone would be impressed by the largeness of his spirit. They would be impressed that he had disdained severity and shown compassion.

In showing mercy to Ben-Hadad, Ahab also demonstrated that he had no appreciation of what the victory had cost in terms of the lives of his soldiers. When Christians fail to heed the warnings of Scripture about peaceful co-existence with the sinfulness of this world (James 4:4), they only show a shocking disregard for the truth that Jesus died to set them free from sin.

The condemnation (20:35-43)

Ahab must have come away from his chariot-consultation feeling very shrewd and proud. The feeling was not to last long. The Lord was not at all pleased with him for showing mercy to Ben-Hadad, and to convey this displeasure he again made use of one of his prophets.

This prophet went about his task in a most unusual way. The Lord first commanded him to solicit a wound from a fellow-prophet (20:35). It was essential for prophets to recognize the Word of the Lord and to obey it promptly. The prophet from whom the wound was solicited failed on both counts and paid with his life for doing so (20:36). We might say the Lord made this prophet a lasting reminder for us to treat the Word of God with the utmost respect. Believers who fail to do so are not killed by lions these days, but their faith and comforts will be eaten by spiritual termites, and they will certainly be brought to account in the hereafter.

The next prophet to whom the same request was addressed immediately complied (20:37), and the first prophet, now wounded and bandaged, stationed himself where he would be sure to encounter Ahab (20:38).

When the king came along, the disguised prophet was ready with a story. He pretended to be a soldier who had in the midst of the battle received from his commanding officer an order, namely, to guard a prisoner. This was a very solemn charge. The soldier would either pay with his life or with a very heavy fine if the prisoner escaped (20:39).

The prisoner did escape, incredibly enough, because of the soldier's carelessness. The soldier did not lose the prisoner because his position was attacked by the enemy, but rather because he was **'busy here and there'** (20:40).

King Ahab felt no compassion for this supposed soldier. As far as he was concerned, there was no reason for compassion.

This man deserved whatever judgement befell him. He knew what he was supposed to do and what the cost would be for failing to do it (20:40), and despite that knowledge he had failed.

Without realizing it Ahab had pronounced judgement upon himself, just as King David had done years before when Nathan the prophet had also spun a story (2 Sam. 12:1-7). Ahab was the man in the prophet's story, even as David was the man in Nathan's story. Although it is not recorded for us, it is evident that Ahab had been given a distinct and solemn charge regarding Ben-Hadad and, through sheer carelessness, he had failed. The Lord had pronounced the death sentence on Ben-Hadad, and Ahab had failed to carry it out even though the Lord had delivered the Syrian king to him. Now Ahab would pay with his life for refusing to take Ben-Hadad's life, and the people of Israel would suffer as well (20:42).

Ahab responded to this blistering prophecy by going to his house in a sullen, sour mood. Ahab was one who blamed others. His problems were always because of others. He could never see that it was his own unfaithfulness to God that created his problems.

Ahab's failure to be a true shepherd to Israel compels us to look to that one who would be a true shepherd to his people, Jesus Christ. His shepherdly concern for his own caused him to lay down his life in their stead (John 10:11-18). While Ahab defeated his own people by embracing their enemy, our Lord, through his atoning death, secured eternal victory for his people by defeating their enemy Satan.

31.
A good man murdered; a bad man sentenced

Please read 1 Kings 21:1-29

A young lad was heard singing the old hymn, 'Rise up, O men of God,' in this way: 'Wise up, O men of God.' Ahab was anything but a man of God, and he certainly never learned to 'wise up'. He had abundant opportunities to observe the havoc and ruin that come from disregarding God's laws, but he went from sin to sin.

In this chapter he embraces yet another sin and stoops to a new low. As far as we know, Ahab had never, prior to this, treated his own subjects with brutality. But he does here. One cannot help but contrast this chapter with what immediately precedes it. There Ahab spared one whom the Lord had sentenced to execution. In this chapter he executes one whom he was not only to spare, but also to protect. He kept the man he was not supposed to keep, and he failed to keep the man he was supposed to keep.

Ahab makes a wicked request (21:1-3)

Ahab had a second palace in Jezreel where he stayed when not in Samaria. Adjoining his property in Jezreel was the vineyard of Naboth. Ahab wanted Naboth to trade or sell the vineyard so he could turn it into a vegetable garden (21:2).

It was a request that Naboth could not honour. The law of God did not allow landowners to dispose of the land allotted to their forefathers except in cases of extreme poverty, and even then the sale was only for the period up to the next jubilee and the land could be redeemed at any time by a close relative who was in a position to do so (Lev. 25:15,23,25; Num. 36:7-9). Ahab probably knew Naboth's land was an original inheritance. He certainly ought to have known what the law said about such land. It was his responsibility as king to govern the people according to the laws of God, but here Ahab encourages one of his subjects to break God's law. God's commandments meant nothing to this man who cared only for his own comfort and pleasure. Is there a connection between Ahab's attitude and the Baal-worship that he had introduced into his kingdom? The author of 1 Kings would answer with an emphatic 'Yes!' He closes this chapter on Ahab's injustice by specifically mentioning his idolatry (21:26). Because the worship of Baal offered sexual rites to gratify the lusts of the flesh, it had become very easy for devotees of Baal to give priority to the gratification of their desires over regard for others.

Ronald S. Wallace writes, 'This story stands here primarily as an illustration of the subtle and radical change that came over the community life of the people of God when they lost touch with the living God, their sense of his reality, and allowed Baal religion to influence their thought and behaviour.'[1]

Naboth was undoubtedly sacrificing a lot to refuse Ahab's offer. Raymond B. Dillard says, 'The expansion of the royal palace was driving up the land values around it. Naboth would have an even better vineyard or could ask for an inflated price; it was also an opportunity to curry royal favour for himself and his family. Who wouldn't take a deal like this? There was everything to gain, and the offer did not seem to have a downside.'[2]

The benefits notwithstanding, Naboth refused. He had such profound reverence for God's law that he would rather sacrifice material profit and risk the wrath of his ruler than disobey. He must have been shocked that his king should even suggest such a thing. His response was swift and sure: **'The LORD forbid that I should give the inheritance of my fathers to you!'** (21:3).

Is there a modern-day parallel to the temptation that came Naboth's way? Christians have in the gospel a treasure that is to be guarded and preserved (1 Tim. 6:20; 2 Tim. 1:13-14). This is no small task. There are many today, like Ahab, who suggest that we sell out. They tell us that times have changed, that no one can be expected to believe in a message that calls them sinners and insists that they are heading for eternal judgement. They tell us that it is more than ludicrous to expect people to look for eternal salvation from a Jewish rabbi who died on a Roman cross two thousand years ago.

The times may have changed, but God has not. He remains the same (Mal. 3:6; Heb. 13:8). And it is not a matter of whether the gospel of Christ suits us, but rather whether it suits him. The fact that he raised Jesus from the grave and seated him at his right hand is all the evidence we need that God is perfectly and eternally satisfied with the gospel of salvation through a crucified Redeemer. We do not, therefore, need a more up-to-date gospel. We need up-to-the-challenge Naboths who refuse to sell out.

Jezebel hatches a foul plot (21:4-16)

Naboth's refusal should have been the end of the matter, but it was not. Ahab stomped off in a rage and, in incredibly child-like fashion, went to his room, where he flung himself on his bed. There he pouted and sulked, staring at the wall and refusing to eat (21:4). Here is the spectacle of a king acting like a spoiled brat!

One cannot help wondering if this behaviour was calculated to arrest the attention of Jezebel and to stir her to take action. If so, it succeeded admirably. Upon learning the reason for his childish behaviour, Jezebel chided him. He was the King of Israel! He did not have to take 'No' for an answer! He could have whatever he wanted! (21:7).

With the promise to secure Naboth's vineyard for her detestable husband, Jezebel, no less detestable than he, set to work. She sent letters to the elders and nobles of the city. These letters, written in Ahab's name and sealed with his seal, called for a fast, as if the city had engaged in terrible sin (21:8-9). The only sin, of course, was the 'sin' Naboth committed when he stood for God's law and against Ahab's request. The letters Jezebel sent also mentioned Naboth. He was to be seated **'with high honour among the people'** (21:9). Some take this to mean that he was to be given a seat of prominence so that he could easily be seen by the false witnesses who were to accuse him. Albert Barnes suggests that the word 'honour' should be omitted and that Jezebel's reference to Naboth's seating should be understood in terms of having him seated before the court as the one who was being charged and tried.[3]

Jezebel's plan was carried out perfectly. The elders and nobles, probably corrupt themselves and certainly in fear of Ahab and Jezebel, convened the fast (21:12). The pre-arranged false witnesses provided testimony that Naboth was guilty of blaspheming God and the king, and Naboth was taken out and stoned (21:13). It is no small irony that, in concocting this scheme, Jezebel adhered to the letter of the law she so despised by arranging for two witnesses (Num. 35:30; Deut. 17:5-6; 19:15). Wicked people are not averse to donning the garb of reverence for God's law if they can further their purposes by doing so.

With Naboth dead, there was no impediment to Ahab's seizing his vineyard. Jezebel's words to her husband, **'Arise, take possession of the vineyard of Naboth the Jezreelite...'** (21:15), must be classified as some of the most vile and hardhearted that have ever fallen from human lips.

The next verse gives us Ahab's response: **'So it was, when Ahab heard that Naboth was dead, that Ahab got up and went down to take possession of the vineyard of Naboth the Jezreelite'** (21:16).

Those words indicate that Ahab was not at all surprised by what Jezebel had done. He certainly felt no pang of conscience about it, but rather sprang from his bed with delight to take possession of his ill-gotten vineyard.

Elijah sentences Ahab (21:17-24)

Ahab's surprise (21:17-20)

God is conspicuous by his absence in the first half of this chapter. Ahab and Jezebel work their wickedness, Naboth lies dead and God is nowhere to be found. All of that abruptly changes. Jezebel no sooner says, 'Arise,' to her husband (21:15) than God says, **'Arise,'** to the prophet Elijah (21:17). God's ways are mysterious to us. We do not understand why he did not intervene in time to spare Naboth's life. But while God's ways are shrouded in mystery, one thing is certain: he will not let sin go unpunished for ever. Ahab was about to learn that he could break God's laws but he could not escape his justice. Elijah the prophet was to confront Ahab while he was strolling in Naboth's vineyard and announce a most fearful and solemn judgement.

The mere sight of Elijah must have given Ahab quite a start. It is likely that he had not laid eyes on the prophet since they parted at the gate of Jezreel (18:46 - 19:3). Perhaps he thought he was finally rid of the prophet, but it was not to be. Elijah stood before him in awful solemnity, and Ahab could only utter a cry which revealed the consciousness of his guilt: **'Have you found me, O my enemy?'** (21:20).

Of course Elijah had found him. He was the servant of the living God from whom nothing is hidden. When someone sells himself to do evil, as Ahab had done (21:20), there is no place to hide. God inevitably finds us, either in salvation or in judgement.

But Ahab was not entirely correct in thinking of Elijah as his enemy. Elijah was his enemy only because Ahab had become the friend of sin. Those who love sin hate the truth and those who declare it. If Ahab had loved the truth, Elijah would have been his best friend. Elijah was even now in a sense befriending Ahab by having the courage to confront him with his sin. The preacher who dares to tell the sinner the truth about his sin is the greatest friend that person could ever have.

Ahab's judgement (21:21-24)

After his initial exchange with the king (21:20), Elijah proceeded to announce the three parts of his devastating message. First, in the same place where dogs had licked the blood of Naboth, dogs would lick Ahab's blood (21:19). Secondly, all the male descendants of Ahab would be destroyed (21:21-22,24). Finally, the dogs would eat Jezebel by the wall of Jezreel (21:23); that is, she would be deprived of burial. It seems that the land itself would reject Jezebel because she had stolen Naboth's land.

The accuracy of Elijah's prophecy regarding Ahab himself is documented in the next chapter (22:38), and the fulfilment of the prophecies regarding his posterity and Jezebel is recorded in 2 Kings 9:1 - 10:17.

Ahab's character (21:25-26)

At this point the author gives us a summation of the character of Ahab. Three distinct details about this despicable man are placed before us. First, he went into wickedness to a very great degree, so much so that it could be said that he **'sold himself'** to sin (21:25). Secondly, much of Ahab's wickedness was due to his weakness. His wife Jezebel constantly **'stirred him up'** to do evil (21:25), and he did not have the will to resist her. Finally, he gave himself to idolatry in a particularly heinous way. He disregarded all the commandments of God about practising the idolatry of the Canaanite nations whom the people of Israel had dispossessed and flung himself into idolatry with abandon (21:26).

Ahab's response (21:27-29)

Having broken in to summarize Ahab's character, the author returns to his narrative by showing how Ahab responded to Elijah's announcement of judgement. He writes, **'So it was, when Ahab heard those words, that he tore his clothes and put sackcloth on his body, and fasted and lay in sackcloth, and went about mourning'** (21:27).

Are we to take these words to mean that Ahab finally came to a genuine repentance? The Lord himself acknowledged that Ahab had **'humbled himself'** before him. And that humbling was genuine enough for the Lord to delay the cutting off of Ahab's descendants (21:29).

But, promising and impressive as Ahab's response was, we have to say it fell short of genuine repentance. This conclusion is forced upon us by his subsequent behaviour. There is no record of his denouncing his wicked wife Jezebel, or seeking to curb her influence in any way. On the other hand, we do find him resorting to four hundred false prophets before going into battle (22:6). And this is what he had to say regarding Micaiah, a true prophet of the Lord: 'I hate him, because he does not prophesy good concerning me, but evil' (22:8). These are hardly the actions and words of one who has genuinely repented.

How, then, are we to explain Ahab's humbling himself after hearing Elijah's message? If this was not true repentance, what was it? It was the temporary expression of a man who had just been hit with a bolt of reality. It was a temporary trembling at the prospect of judgement. But while Ahab feared judgement and wanted to escape it, he did not hate the sin that prompted the judgement.

This raises yet another question: if Ahab's repentance was not sincere, why did God delay his judgement? In so doing, the Lord revealed something of the greatness of his mercy. Matthew Henry draws this conclusion from the Lord's treatment of Ahab's insincere repentance: 'If a pretending partial penitent shall go to his house reprieved, doubtless a sincere penitent shall go to his house justified.'[4]

The story of Naboth losing his vineyard to the vile Ahab, while very sad and tragic, gives those who know the Lord reasons to rejoice. The children of God have, through the work of Christ, received an inheritance that cannot be taken away. It is an inheritance that is '... incorruptible and undefiled and that does not fade away.' It is 'reserved' in heaven for God's people (1 Peter 1:4).

32.
The Lord's sentence executed

Please read 1 Kings 22:1-40

The prophet Elijah pronounced sentence upon Ahab in Naboth's vineyard. The chapter to which we now come relates the execution of that sentence. Here Ahab hears the same sentence of death from yet another prophet of the Lord, Micaiah, and here he dies, and both prophecies are fulfilled. His sentence of death was irreversible and inescapable.

This chapter presents a vital message for our time. The Word of God is often disregarded and disdained these days, but it will finally be vindicated. We can no more escape it than Ahab did. If we treat its message with contempt, as he did, we shall most certainly experience the fearful sentence of doom it pronounces upon the ungodly. The Word of God shall triumph.

The Lord had not only determined that Ahab should die because of his wickedness, but also that he should die in a certain way. If the dogs were to lick his blood, as Elijah had promised (21:19), it was essential for Ahab to die from a severe wound. 1 Kings 22 shows us how the Lord brought all this about. It disturbs many because it claims that God made use of **'a lying spirit'** to bring about Ahab's death (22:20-23). This was the flat affirmation of the prophet Micaiah who holds centre stage in this chapter. Let's consider the prelude to Micaiah's prophecy, the prophecy itself and the results of it.

The prelude to Micaiah's prophecy (22:1-12)

Ahab's desire to reclaim Ramoth-Gilead (22:1-4)

The chapter opens with Ahab enlisting Jehoshaphat, King of Judah, to join him in repossessing the city of Ramoth in Gilead (22:3). This city, one of those Moses designated as a city of refuge for unintentional killers (Deut. 4:43; Josh. 20:8), was located east of the Jordan river in north-eastern Gilead. It had been taken from Israel by the Syrians and Ahab wanted it back. Some commentators think Ahab expected his treaty with Ben-Hadad (20:34) to result in this city's being returned to Israel. Ahab was now hoping to accomplish with military action what he had failed to accomplish through the treaty.

Tensions between Israel and Judah had eased to the point where the two kings were now allied by the marriage of Ahab's daughter to Jehoshaphat's son. Jehoshaphat's treaty with Ahab probably obligated him to share in military campaigns and, as a man of integrity who kept his commitments, he agreed to share in the venture (22:4). In the next chapter, we shall find Jehoshaphat being rebuked for associating with the wicked Ahab.

The false prophecy of 400 prophets (22:5-12)

Complying with Jehoshaphat's request for guidance from the Lord on this matter, Ahab commanded 400 prophets to come before him and Jehoshaphat, and asked whether military action should be taken against Ramoth Gilead. And the prophets to a man said, **'Go up, for the Lord will deliver it into the hand of the king'** (22:6).

This must have been quite a scene to behold: two kings in their finery, 400 prophets chanting their victory chorus (22:12) and one prophet, Zedekiah, running about with horns to gore imaginary Syrians (22:11). This scene reminds us that great numbers and great enthusiasm do not mean that people are truly meeting with God or hearing from him.

Jehoshaphat was not impressed. He knew these prophets were hired by Ahab for this very purpose. They were 'yes men' who were much more concerned about pleasing the king than preaching the truth. While these men spoke in the name of the Lord, the truth is that they were not even prophets of the Lord. They were probably prophets of the religion Jeroboam had put in place (12:25-33). This religion, while ostensibly honouring the God of Israel, was in reality a total departure from him. This did not, however, keep these prophets from tossing the name of the Lord around with great ease.

Jehoshaphat wanted to hear from a man to whom God spoke so forcefully that he himself could not help but speak that word to others, a man in whom the word of the Lord burned so fiercely that he disdained both popularity and political pressure. There were not many such men in Ahab's kingdom. Elijah was one, but Ahab does not even mention him. It may be that Elijah, so notorious for being difficult to find and for showing up only when he desired to do so, was omitted because Ahab assumed it would be impossible to locate him.

Then there was Micaiah. We have not met him prior to this, although some think he may very well have been the unnamed prophet who condemned Ahab after the latter made the treaty with Ben-Hadad (20:35-43). After expressing his hatred for Micaiah (22:8), Ahab yielded to Jehoshaphat's request and sent for him (22:9).

These developments reveal that, while Ahab and Jehoshaphat were allied politically, they were poles apart spiritually. The former had demonstrated time and time again that he had no regard for God. Ahab was a user of religion. If religion could further his designs and achieve his goals, he was happy to tip his hat to it. Baal-worship, Jeroboam's cult, or even, on occasions such as this, paying lip-service to the true God — it did not matter to Ahab as long as it served his own ends. It is doubtful whether Ahab believed in anything at all except his own power, pleasure and comfort.

The prophecy of Micaiah (22:13-28)

Micaiah's first words to Ahab make it appear that he had wavered in his resolve to speak only the word of the Lord (22:14). When Ahab asked him if he should attack Ramoth Gilead, he said, **'Go and prosper, for the Lord will deliver it into the hand of the king'** (22:15).

The subsequent exchange shows that Micaiah, far from wavering, was only being sarcastic. It was as if he said to Ahab, 'You don't want to hear the truth, so I won't tell you the truth.'

The vision of the death of Ahab (22:17-18)

Micaiah was correct. Ahab didn't want the truth. But this time the king, recognizing the prophet's sarcasm and intent on proving to Jehoshaphat that the prophet had only evil to say about him, urged Micaiah to speak the truth (22:16,18).

Micaiah immediately complied by saying, **'I saw all Israel scattered on the mountains, as sheep that have no shepherd. And the Lord said, "These men have no master. Let each return to his house in peace"'** (22:17). There was no room for doubt about Micaiah's meaning. Ahab was to die in the battle for Ramoth-Gilead.

The vision of the lying spirit (22:19-23)

Micaiah had even more to say. He had been enabled to peer into the throne room of God and to hear what was said there.

From what he had seen and heard, Micaiah could say that Ahab was about to die in battle because the Lord designed it to be so. His 400 prophets had been possessed with a lying spirit so Ahab would be persuaded to go into battle (22:19-23). This lying spirit is not to be identified with God or any of his heavenly host, who are pure and holy, but rather with Satan himself, who appeared before God as we find him doing in the first chapter of Job (Job 1:6-12).[1]

The fact that God allowed Satan to deceive Ahab through false prophets does not mean that God is the author of evil, or that he in any way approves of it. It rather reminds us that God can use evil to accomplish his purposes. Scripture provides us with several examples of this. God certainly did not approve of the evil Joseph's brothers committed when they sold him into slavery, but he used that evil for good (Gen. 50:20). God did not approve of the evil of the Babylonian Empire, but he used that empire to chastise his people. God did not approve of the evil of the men who crucified Jesus, but he used it to provide eternal salvation for his people.

The Lord of truth judges those who hate his truth. Ahab and his prophets loved lies, so the Lord permitted Satan to give them a lie to love. It must be noted that God also gave them his truth through Micaiah but, faced with the two, the king and his prophets showed their true colours by embracing the lie.

The results of Micaiah's prophecy (22:24-40)

Persecution for Micaiah (22:24-28)

Zedekiah took special umbrage at Micaiah's words about the lying spirit. He could not believe that the spirit of the Lord would bypass him to speak to Micaiah and, thoroughly enraged, he slapped Micaiah's cheek (22:24). The latter may very well have thought this to be a small price to pay when he stopped to consider that he could have been gored! (22:11).

Ahab liked Micaiah's message no better than Zedekiah did and responded by commanding that the prophet be jailed until his return from battle (22:27). Micaiah retorted: **'If you ever return in peace, the LORD has not spoken by me'** (22:28). In his last recorded words we see him holding high the Mosaic standard for all prophets, that is, the fulfilment of their prophecies (Deut. 18:21-22).

The responses of Zedekiah and Ahab reflect a truth writ large in Scripture — that those who dare to declare God's truth will find in the hearts of men a readiness to despise that truth and those who declare it. It is a costly thing to stand for truth in a time which prizes error.

Death for Ahab (22:29-40)

The fact that Micaiah's prophecy so powerfully repeated what Ahab had already heard from Elijah makes us wonder why the king was prepared to go into battle. Ronald S. Wallace offers this analysis: 'At this stage of his life, so hardened had Ahab become against God and his laws, that instead of deterring him, his word provoked defiance. It now added a new dimension to his purpose in going to Ramoth Gilead. He was no longer out merely to teach the King of Aram a lesson and to win the city, he was out also, and primarily, to teach the prophets of God a lesson, and to express the scorn he was now feeling for them. All his life he had been frustrated by their word... Now he has his opportunity to end their rule of superstition. His expedition will be victorious and when he returns he will expose their sham.'[2]

An even harder question is why Jehoshaphat was prepared to go into battle after hearing from Micaiah. There seems to be no definitive answer for this. The fact that he had given his word coupled with the fact that the prophet had spoken only of the death of Ahab may have emboldened him to see the matter through. Belief in the justness of reclaiming Ramoth Gilead may also have contributed to his decision.

Ahab thought he could prevent the fulfilment of Micaiah's prophecy by going into battle in disguise (22:29-30). It appeared at first that his ruse would work, but it finally proved to be as ineffective here as it did when Jeroboam and his wife tried it (14:1-6). Ben-Hadad, whom Ahab had so leniently spared at Aphek (20:31-34), was in no mood to return the favour. He commanded his soldiers to focus on killing the King of Israel (22:31). Expecting Ahab to be in his royal attire, they mistakenly focused on Jehoshaphat (22:32-33).

While the Syrians could be deceived, God could not. He did not need Ahab to be attired as a king, or the Syrians to specifically focus on killing him. **'A certain man drew a bow at random, and struck the king of Israel...'** (22:34), and Ahab was mortally wounded. Matthew Henry aptly notes: 'Those cannot escape with life whom God hath doomed to death.'[3]

Some would explain it in terms of chance, but this was the hand of God. He guided the hand that pulled the bow and guided the arrow so that it struck in exactly the right spot. Such is his sovereign control over human events. And such is his faithfulness to his Word. The prophecy of Micaiah came true with the random shot of the archer, and the prophecy of Elijah came true with the dogs licking Ahab's blood in the same place where they licked the blood of Naboth, that is, at **'a pool in Samaria'** (22:38). Some argue that Elijah's prophecy did not come true because Naboth died in Jezreel and the dogs licked Ahab's blood 'in Samaria' (22:38). It is entirely conceivable, however, that the pool referred to in this verse was called 'The Pool of Samaria,' and that it was located in Jezreel. Many towns today have streets named after other towns, so it is not unreasonable to suppose that Jezreel may have had a pool named after Samaria. Furthermore, it makes sense that Ahab's servants would have stopped at Jezreel to wash out the king's bloody chariot before proceeding to Samaria to bury him.[4]

Ahab did not like Micaiah's message, but it came true. Many today reject the historic Christian faith because they do not like its emphasis on the guilt of sin, the certainty of judgement, the reality of hell and the necessity of repentance. They are further offended when they are told that there is only one way of eternal salvation, and that way is through the bloody death of Jesus Christ on a Roman cross. As far as they are concerned, if people do need eternal salvation, there has to be a better way than this.

Those who are put off by biblical Christianity easily identify with the slogan used by one religious denomination: 'Instead of me fitting a religion, I found a religion to fit me.' Ahab had in his court prophets a message that 'fitted' him, but their message cost him his life. Those who jettison the historic Christian gospel to embrace a message of their own liking may find temporary comfort in doing so, but will find themselves eternally separated from God.

33.
Light in Judah; darkness in Israel

Please read 1 Kings 22:41-53

1 Kings comes to a close with brief summaries of the reign of Jehoshaphat in Judah and the reign of Ahab's son, Ahaziah, in Israel. These summaries about two kings and two kingdoms constitute a very fitting end for this part of the author's story. The division of the kingdom into two parts is, after all, the primary development in 1 Kings.

The few verses of these summaries show in a very telling way the vast difference between the two kingdoms. The kingdom of Israel had an unbroken line of evil kings, while the kingdom of Judah enjoyed from time to time kings who were faithful to the Lord. The reigns of these godly kings enabled the kingdom of Judah to survive Israel by 136 years.

The light of Jehoshaphat in Judah (22:41-50)

Jehoshaphat was one of Judah's eight godly kings. Beginning his reign in the fourth year of Ahab's reign over Israel, he reigned twenty-five years (22:41-42). A much fuller account of his reign is recorded in 2 Chronicles chapters 17, 19 and 20.

For his part, the author of 1 Kings is content to emphasize the obedience that primarily characterized Jehoshaphat's reign while noting two areas of failure.

Jehoshaphat's obedience (22:43,46)

The author describes Jehoshaphat's obedience to the Lord by saying he **'walked in all the ways of his father Asa'** (22:43). Asa had carried out a programme of vigorous reform out of a heart that was 'loyal to the LORD' (15:14). These reforms included banishing many of the cult prostitutes from the land, removing the idols his fathers had introduced and deposing his grandmother Maachah from being queen mother because of the obscene image she had made (15:12-13). Jehoshaphat followed in his father's footsteps by removing the remaining cult prostitutes (22:46). All of this was **'right in the eyes of the LORD'** (22:43).

Jehoshaphat's failures (22:43-44,48-49)

With all the good Jehoshaphat did, there was still a **'nevertheless'** (22:43) and an **'also'** to be added (22:44).

The high places. The **'nevertheless'** arose from Jehoshaphat's failure to eliminate the **'high places'** from the land. This statement appears to contradict the claim of 2 Chronicles that Jehoshaphat did indeed remove the high places (2 Chr. 17:6). Howard F. Vos writes of these apparently conflicting statements: 'This must indicate either that he removed some of the more important ones but did not fully clear the country of them, or that he removed them once but the people restored them and he did not remove them a second time.'[1]

   John Gill's explanation is more compelling. He contends that Jehoshaphat '... took away the high places and groves for idolatrous worship ... but not the high places in which sacrifices were offered to the Lord, which ought to have been, especially since the temple was built'.[2]

In all likelihood Jehoshaphat found these high places very difficult to eliminate because they were so popular. We are living in days in which all kinds of adjustments are being made in public worship with one thing alone in mind, namely, what the worshippers find to be pleasant, appealing and exciting. The Lord's displeasure with the high places that were supposed to be for him shows us that he demands that we worship him, not as it pleases us, but rather as it pleases him. When we try to be sovereign in the area of worship, we intrude into a realm that God has reserved for himself.

By driving the money-changers and merchants out of the temple, the Lord Jesus showed that he is sovereign on this matter of worship. He highly values worship and insists that it be done in the right way (John 2:13-22).

The unholy alliances. The **'also'** brings us to Jehoshaphat's second notable failure: his unholy alliances. The author tells us that Jehoshaphat **'made peace with the king of Israel'** (22:44), that is, with Ahab. This was accomplished in part by Jehoshaphat's arranging for his son to marry the daughter of Ahab (2 Kings 8:16-18; 2 Chr. 18:1).

Such an alliance undoubtedly appeared to Jehoshaphat to be nothing more than a shrewd political move. It reduced tensions and diminished the prospect of war. But a policy that makes political sense does not necessarily please the Lord. When Jehoshaphat returned from the battle in which Ahab was killed, he was met by Jehu, the son of Hanani. Jehu had this stern message for the king: 'Should you help the wicked and love those who hate the LORD? Therefore the wrath of the LORD is upon you. Nevertheless good things are found in you, in that you have removed the wooden images from the land, and have prepared your heart to seek God' (2 Chr. 19:2-3).

Jehu's words were not overblown. Ahab did indeed hate
the Lord, and it was very strange and unseemly for the godly
Jehoshaphat to be allied with him. But Jehoshaphat did not
take the prophet's words to heart, at least not in a permanent
way, because he later 'allied himself with Ahaziah king of Israel, who acted very wickedly' (2 Chr. 20:35).

This alliance with Ahab's son was for the purpose of building ships. It undoubtedly made good sense economically, but
the Lord was no more pleased with it than he was with
Jehoshaphat's alliance with Ahab himself. Because of his displeasure the Lord sent yet another prophet to Jehoshaphat
with this message: 'Because you have allied yourself with
Ahaziah, the LORD has destroyed your works' (2 Chr. 20:37).
The Chronicler notes the fulfilment of the prophet's words by
adding this comment: 'Then the ships were wrecked, so that
they were not able to go to Tarshish' (2 Chr. 20:37).

Truths of continuing validity

The Lord's unhappiness with Jehoshaphat's alliances is not
just a slice of antiquity that has no meaning or value for us. It
rather displays for us two major truths: the need for God's
people to separate themselves from the world and the reality
of the Lord's chastisement in the lives of his people.

Separation from the world

When God calls his people to himself he calls them to be different from the world and to be like himself. The apostle Paul
strikes the note of separation in these words:

> Come out from among them
> And be separate, says the Lord.

> Do not touch what is unclean,
> And I will receive you
>
> (2 Cor. 6:17).

The apostle Peter sounds the call for the people of the Lord to be like the Lord: '... as he who called you is holy, you also be holy in all your conduct, because it is written, "Be holy, for I am holy"' (1 Peter 1:15-16).

The Bible does not call for Christians to shut themselves off completely from the world. We are to be in the world but not of it (John 17:15-16). It rather calls us to realize as we live in this world that we are citizens of another world (Phil. 3:20), and to take our orders from the King of that world and to reflect his likeness.

We can take this matter of separation a step further. Our commitment to maintaining separation from the world is to be so firm that we must be willing to separate ourselves even from churches and Christian organizations that have become permeated with worldly thinking and doing (1 Cor. 5:11; 10:21-22).

In allying himself with the kings of Israel, Jehoshaphat was essentially saying differences in religious beliefs do not matter. He was allying himself with kings and with a nation who had given themselves over to the worship of false gods, while he himself was a worshipper of the true God. If the adherents of the modern-day ecumenical movement are correct in their call for Christians to minimize doctrine and ally themselves with each other, we would expect to read that the Lord was pleased with Jehoshaphat's early attempt at ecumenism. But he was not pleased. The Lord puts a premium on the truth of his Word, and he is never pleased with those who barter that truth away, even if it is in the name of unity. The Lord ever calls us to fellowship around the truths of his Word.

The apostle Paul had the opportunity to put unity ahead of truth when his fellow-apostle Peter compromised the truth of the gospel by refusing to eat with Gentile believers at Antioch. Paul could not let such compromise go unchallenged. He says of Peter, 'I withstood him to his face, because he was to be blamed' (Gal. 2:11). Paul knew it is better to be divided by truth than to be united in error. He knew it is better to speak truth that hurts and then heals than to speak falsehood that comforts and then kills. He knew it is better to be hated for telling the truth than to be loved for telling a lie. He knew it is better to stand alone for truth than to stand with a multitude in error. All who are enamoured with the ecumenism that downplays doctrinal differences for the sake of unity would do well to think deeply about Paul's zeal for the truth.

The Lord's chastisement

God is pro-active with his people. He did not sit idly by while Jehoshaphat associated with Ahab and Ahaziah. He first, as we have noted, sent the prophet Jehu to Jehoshaphat. He then sent chastisement in the form of wrecked ships.

The Lord is the Father of his people and, as any good father chastens his children, so the Lord chastens his people. He does not chasten out of a desire to be cruel and harsh, but rather out of concern and love for his people. Through chastening he weans them away from the things of this world and causes them to grow and mature spiritually. Chastening is for their good, because God's people find their greatest happiness in being brought close to the Lord.

God's chastening was effective in the life of Jehoshaphat. The author of 1 Kings notes that he refused when Ahaziah approached him about yet another joint venture in shipping (22:49).

The darkness of Ahaziah in Israel (22:51-53)

Triple wickedness and double idolatry

The author follows his summary of the reign of Jehoshaphat with a small capsule regarding Ahaziah. While obedience was the rule for Jehoshaphat and disobedience the exception, just the opposite was the case with Ahaziah. During his two-year reign, Ahaziah indulged in such wicked living that the author of 1 Kings could only describe it by piling one dreadful description on another. We might say Ahaziah was a man of 'triple' wickedness and 'double' idolatry. Here is his triple wickedness: he walked in the way of his father Ahab, in the way of his mother Jezebel and in the way of Israel's first king Jeroboam (22:52).

This threefold path led to double idolatry. Ahaziah continued the worship of Jeroboam's calves right along with the worship of Baal.

What does all this have to do with us? Jeroboam's calves and Baal have disappeared, but idolatry remains. It is certainly more subtle and sophisticated than in Ahaziah's time, but it is just as real. Raymond B. Dillard observes: 'Human beings seem ever ready and willing to trust in idols. Today we may not stand in front of statues made by human hands, but we have plenty of other idols. Idols are those things we serve in order to establish and maintain our own sense of wholeness and well-being. Idols in our lives are often money and material things, jobs, power, position, influence, and even other people.'[3]

God's ever-watching eye

The author wants us to understand that Ahaziah's evil was done **'in the sight of the LORD'** (22:52). God is the unrelenting, never-sleeping watcher of human events and the discerner of human hearts. Nothing is hidden from him. These truths are hammered home in Scripture after Scripture. Nowhere is it stated more pungently than by the author of Hebrews: 'And there is no creature hidden from his sight, but all things are naked and open to the eyes of him to whom we must give account' (Heb. 4:13).

God's anger against sin

The author also wants us to understand that Ahaziah's sin **'provoked the LORD God of Israel to anger'** (22:53). The Lord is not casual and unconcerned about the sin he sees. His holy character does not allow him to be casual and nonchalant about it. Sin provokes him to anger. Nothing is more disconcerting to modern ears than to hear of the anger of God. People often respond to this assertion by saying, 'My God is a God of love.' We should never in any way diminish or denigrate the love of God. Thank God for his love! But neither should we elevate that attribute of God above all other attributes. The reality is that God never loves at the expense of his holiness or through compromising his holiness. All we have to do to see this is look at the death of Jesus on the cross. Yes, it was a marvellous expression of the love of God, but it was at one and the same time a satisfaction of the justice and holiness of God. God did not merely say through that cross, 'Look at how much I love you!' He also said, 'Look at how much I hate your sin!' The cross was a perfect blending of the love and justice of God. The justice of God was there because God judged the sins of his people in the person of his Son. The love of God was there because he certainly did not have to do this. The cross is not God letting sinners off the hook. It is God putting himself on the hook on their behalf.

Because God has justly dealt with sin in the death of Christ on the cross, no penalty remains for the believing sinner. But those who stubbornly cling to their sins will have to bear that penalty. It all comes down to this: God's anger against our sin was either spent on Christ on the cross, or it will be spent on us in eternity.

The short description of Ahaziah allows us to see how incredibly hard the human heart can be. Ahaziah had seen where the idolatry of Jeroboam had led. He had also seen where the idolatry of his father had led. He would soon hear a frightful message from Elijah about where his own idolatry would lead (2 Kings 1), but, with it all, he refused to turn to the Lord, and thus went into eternity bearing his own sin.

Notes

Introduction
1. Gleason L. Archer, Jr., *A Survey of Old Testament Introduction,* Moody Press, p.289.
2. Terence E. Fretheim, *First and Second Kings,* Westminster John Knox Press, p.10.
3. As above, p.8.
4. David M. Howard, Jr., *An Introduction to the Old Testament Historical Books,* Moody Press, 1993.
5. Fretheim, *First and Second Kings,* p.5.
6. The author's references in 8:8 to the poles of the ark being in the temple 'to this day' and in 9:21 to Solomon's conscripting a labour force 'to this day' seem to militate against the view that he was writing during the Babylonian Captivity. Evangelical commentators solve this problem by pointing to the absence of the phrase 'to this day' from the oldest manuscripts, or by suggesting that the author simply carried into his writing a quotation from another source.

Chapter 1 — God's purpose prevailing
1. Ronald S. Wallace, *Readings in 1 Kings,* William B. Eerdmans Publishing Co., p.6.
2. As above, p.8.
3. Charles Spurgeon, *Treasury of David,* MacDonald Publishing Co., vol. i, p.11.

Chapter 2 — Solomon established
1. Howard F. Vos, *Bible Study Commentary: 1,2 Kings,* Zondervan Publishing House, p.39.
2. As above.
3. Wallace, *Readings,* p.19.
4. As above.

Chapter 3 — A good beginning
1. Brian L. Harbour, *From Cover to Cover,* Broadman Press, p.62.

Chapter 4 — Solomon in all his glory
1. R. D. Patterson, *The Expositor's Bible Commentary: 1 and 2 Kings,* vol. iv, Zondervan Publishing House, p.50.
2. Vos, *1,2 Kings,* p.50.
3. Archer, *Survey,* p.467.
4. As above.
5. Matthew Henry, *Matthew Henry's Commentary,* Fleming H. Revell Publishing Co., vol. ii, p.599.
6. As above.
7. S. G. DeGraaf, *Promise and Deliverance,* vol. ii, Presbyterian and Reformed Publishing Co., p.200.
8. Derek Kidner, *Tyndale Old Testament Commentaries: Psalms 1-71,* Inter-Varsity Press, p.254.
9. Jonathan Edwards, *The Works of Jonathan Edwards,* vol. i, p.557.

Chapter 6 — Solomon the builder
1. Michael Wilcock, *The Bible Speaks Today: The Message of Chronicles,* Inter-Varsity Press, p.133.
2. John MacArthur, ed., *The MacArthur Study Bible,* Word Bibles, p.480.
3. John Gill, *Exposition of the Old and New Testaments,* vol. ii, p.696.
4. As above.
5. Eugene H. Merrill, *Bible Study Commentary: 1,2 Chronicles,* Zondervan Publishing House, p.94.
6. As above.
7. Vos, *1,2 Kings,* p.39.

Chapter 7 — A special day
1. Patterson, *1 and 2 Kings,* p.80.
2. A. W. Pink, *Gleanings in Exodus,* Moody Press, p.204.
3. Vos, *1,2 Kings,* p.67.

Chapter 9 — With Solomon in the school of prayer
1. Harbour, *Cover to Cover,* p.170.
2. Paul House, *New American Commentary, 1,2 Kings,* Broadman Press, vol. viii, p.144.

Chapter 11 — Manifold blessings
1. Patterson, *1 and 2 Kings,* p.95.

Chapter 12 — The Queen of Sheba
1. Alexander Maclaren, *Expositions of Holy Scripture,* Baker Book House, vol. ii, p.196.

2. Charles Spurgeon, *Metropolitan Tabernacle Pulpit,* Pilgrim Publications, vol. xlviii, pp.221-5.

Chapter 13 — The turning-point
1. DeGraaf, *Promise,* p.216.
2. As above, p.217.

Chapter 15 — Human folly and divine sovereignty
1. Wallace, *Readings,* p.80.
2. As above, p.85.
3. DeGraaf, *Promise,* p. 225.

Chapter 16 — Jeroboam's folly
1. House, *1,2 Kings,* p.185.

Chapter 17 — A hard-hitting prophet and a hard-hearted king
1. House, *1,2 Kings,* p.205.
2. As above, p.189.

Chapter 18 — The tenacity of the Word of God
1. Fretheim, *First and Second Kings,* p.79.
2. As above.

Chapter 19 — Jeroboam, Mrs Jeroboam and a blind prophet
1. Patterson, *1 and 2 Kings,* p.123.
2. Gill, *Exposition,* vol. ii, p.736.
3. Donald J. Wiseman, *The Tyndale Old Testament Commentaries: 1 and 2 Kings,* Inter-Varsity Press, p.150.

Chapter 21 — A powerful reign with a pitiful end
1. Gill, *Exposition,* vol. ii, p.739.

Chapter 22 — Vital lessons from vile kings
1. Cited by O. S. Hawkins, *Moral Earthquakes and Secret Faults,* Broadman & Holman Publishers, p.30.

Chapter 23 — Elijah before Ahab and at Cherith
1. House, *1,2 Kings,* p.211.
2. MacArthur, *Study Bible,* p.503.

Chapter 24 — Elijah at the widow's house
1. Roger Ellsworth, *Standing for God: The Story of Elijah,* The Banner of Truth Trust, p.42.
2. Cited in House, *1,2 Kings,* p.215.

Chapter 28 — Elijah renewed and recommissioned
1. MacArthur, *Study Bible,* p.507.

Chapter 29 — Ahab defeats the Syrians
1. Wallace, *Readings,* pp.142-3.
2. As above, p.150.

Chapter 30 — Ahab defeats Syria — and Israel!
1. Wallace, *Readings,* p.144.
2. As above.
3. Vos, *1,2 Kings,* p.126.
4. Wiseman, *1 and 2 Kings,* p.178.
5. Vos, *1 and 2 Kings,* p.178.

Chapter 31 — A good man murdered; a bad man sentenced
1. Wallace, *Readings,* pp.152-3.
2. Raymond B. Dillard, *Faith in the Face of Apostasy,* P & R Publishing, p.68.
3. Albert Barnes, *Barnes 'Notes on the Old & New Testaments: 1 Samuel-Esther,* p.217.
4. Henry, *Commentary,* p.699.

Chapter 32 — The Lord's sentence executed
1. Gill, *Exposition,* vol. ii, p.767.
2. Wallace, *Readings,* p.168.
3. Henry, *Commentary,* p.705.
4. Gleason Archer, *Encyclopedia of Bible Difficulties,* Zondervan Publishing House, pp.201-2.

Chapter 33 — Light in Judah; darkness in Israel
1. Vos, *1,2 Kings,* pp.134-5.
2. Gill, *Exposition,* vol. ii, p.770.
3. Dillard, *Faith,* p.30.